# a written self-portrait
## "On Psychosis"

A Novella

By Louis Gale

Vol. I

ISBN 978-1-63784-507-3 (paperback)
ISBN 978-1-63784-639-1 (hardcover)
ISBN 978-1-63784-508-0 (digital)



Hawes & Jenkins Publishing
16427 N Scottsdale Road Suite 410
Scottsdale, AZ 85254
www.hawesjenkins.com

Printed in the United States of America

For you

"I found this very disturbing and don't ever want to hear from you again!"

—family member

"It's very interesting and I can't wait to read more!"

—family member

"I have definitely been THERE before, emotionally speaking that it is."

—friends

"Seems like this could almost be a thesis or dissertation of some kind."

—anonymous

"So, you're saying that each letter has its own pattern of information; open for interpretation?"

—science

"Why do people think this has ANYTHING to do with you?"

—fiction

"An extremely exaggerated exaggeration of any particular emotion"

—feeling

"Whatever…"

—god

# Acknowledgments

If I've met you … even the briefest of
encounters … Thank you.

# Introduction

Wilshire Blvd never had such a glow. I mean, Los Angeles at night always has that orange haze, but tonight in Santa Monica, the beginning of Wilshire, or the end depending on your perspective, the glow was exceptional. It's 10:33 on a Sunday night. It's interesting, driving around LA at night; you always get the clarity you need. That's why I'm out – I need clarity, and for whatever reasons, traffic is the antithesis to clarity. I still don't get why people get so upset during traffic - it's only slowing you down. Maybe it's keeping you from dying in a car accident, or preventing some other shitty thing from happening to you, so... I usually welcome it. Then again, here I am, avoiding the traffic, avoiding my potential SLOW DOWN moment, so who knows what the fuck is going on in the universe. God, I really am one of those people who look deeply into random events and feel they have some spiritual or higher level meaning: That is, if I choose to acknowledge that meaning, which I usually do, so yes of course life can be pretty shitty at times - or pretty great, depending on perspective. Great because I never have any issues with control: people come people go, friends come friends go, family lives family dies – it's all part of the GRAND ORDER of chaotic control, as I like to call it. Shitty at times because, well, it's the same: people come people go, friends come friends go, family lives family dies. It really is all the same. Shitty or great, each side of the spectrum is no different than the other. Happy or sad, success or failure, love and hate; it's ALL THE SAME! There is a control to the universe, but it's chaotic, therefore we must *let go of control!*

Wow, I sound like one of those new age hippies that I despise so much. I wish I actually thought like this, unfortunately I don't. I used to, so at least there was a time when I was free from the tyranny of my own thoughts, but now my mind just runs wild. Then again, since I now ACCEPT the fact that my mind runs wild, and I'm no longer trying to silence it, it almost seems as though I have MORE control. I'm in control of the fact that I have absolutely no control over my own thoughts, and this has become my new religion: whatever I think, I actually think. It's thinking about my thinking. I think therefore I think. It's better to have think and thought, than never to have think-thought before. Yes, I know, I have issues.

And to back track, it's not that I despise new age hippy people, it's that I despise MOST PEOPLE. Especially those who cling to ideas and feel that from their appearance they must represent those ideas: Hippies, new agers and pretty much everybody in the world – all represent their ideas through appearances. Especially hippies, which was a movement in the sixties, my mom was a hippie for Christ sake, she's 67 now. It was that generation, so why the hell are you trying to represent that in today's world, especially by wearing the exact same clothes they did. You're not about peace and love, you're not, and I know that, so please stop thinking you are - Here, I'll tell you what you are, since we're in my mind and it really doesn't matter what I think or say because I'm the only one enjoying this – YOU'RE LOST!

Sure you can take drugs to search the depths of your soul in the quest to find the meaning in your life, but I'll tell you, it's all in vain – you have no meaning in your life and that's why you have to take drugs to go searching in the first place. I love my mom more than anything because she was a TRUE hippie, embodying the essence of what this life is about – Love, and that's how she raised me – with unconditional TRUE love. But she doesn't go prancing around with hula hoops, and walking around bare foot all day. I mean, she used too, but that was in the 60'S! When it actually meant something, living in the past is like eating breakfast for dinner, it only makes sense when your DRUNK and leaving the club.

But back to the love, since it seems I'm lacking it, but in truth: I have too much love, and therein lay the problem. I live in a world, with its many "types" trying to show they are the embodiment of this love by simply wearing it on their sleeve – Love is art, and art is truth, hence LOVE IS TRUTH. The homeless person on the street using cardboard as his canvas is more of an artist than the hippie chick, who searches her soul in vain, to find meaning. You can't look to find meaning. Meaning is something that finds you. By taking a quest to find who you are, you actually remove yourself from the path that's designed that will eventually provide all of the meaning you need to actually find who you are. *Letting the path find you is the hard-*

*est quest you can ever take.* It requires doing nothing, and for whatever reason, people feel that by doing nothing, nothing happens, and when nothing happens people start searching, and when people start searching, they look to fill a void, and when you have a void, you always look to fill it. That's backwards though, because by doing nothing, nothing is left undone, and if nothing is left undone, everything is done, so there's no need to search, since there's nothing to search for, and if there's nothing to search for, there's no need to fill a void since you have no void to begin with. To put it simply, which I love doing: *Let it be*, thank you John Lennon.

Okay, I'm a little hard on the hippies, but it's only because they're the epitome of what spreading your values through appearances represent.

That, and of course, I dated a hippie chick for a while and she's the only girl to actually break my heart. I mean, who in their right mind wouldn't want to be with me! That's obviously rhetorical. But really, especially a hippy chick who's SUPPOSED TO BE acknowledging the ways of the universe – I don't think you can get more of a universal sign than finding FOUR, four leaf clovers on a first date. And not even a typical date – a skate date – it rhymes, it has harmony, it's a sign! But apparently not, "In due time" she says, and just like that, heartbroken.

There is no "due time," time is now! And for you to think that there is a potential due time, well I know I made the right decision not seeing you after that. I mean, you even gave me your frog painting within a month of seeing you!

Well here's something you didn't know – I DID KNOW what it was – the moment I touched it I knew exactly what my Christmas gift was. In fact, I knew once I saw the frog painting hanging in your kitchen that I would be getting that from you - I hate saying it, but I know things. And one of the things I knew, in addition to getting the painting: I knew we would NEVER have sex. Because what you couldn't understand about me, and it's why I decided we wouldn't have sex, is that sex is actually a bigger thing for ME than it is for you. Sure I've gone through my man whore stages, most guys do – but that doesn't mean I didn't wake up crying, hating myself for doing what I wish I could be doing with only ONE AMAZING GIRL. And that's what I've been searching for: that one amazing girl. And once I find her, once I'm with her intimately – that's it for me! I'll never need another girl again. And as hot as you were, and that's all you really were, a beautiful shell, but like so many shells on the beach – you're empty inside, so how on earth could you possibly be that one amazing girl? You're simply not!

And the part of reality you really couldn't see: once you thought I didn't know what my Christmas gift was, and I had to fake a reaction to coincide with your FAKE REALITY, I knew exactly what this relationship was – a detour. Not that a detour is bad, it was probably the best left turn I ever took in my life. So good in fact that I'm pretty sure it was a right turn, it only seems left from my perspective; but looking at a left turn from across the way – *left is always right*! And that's what it is, I can't keep looking at where I'm going while I'm on my way to get there – it's only after the experiment is finished that we can then understand what the results represent. I've always had to know the results prematurely, which only taints the experiment, therefore never understanding what the TRUE results are. I mean, whatever they are, they're ALWAYS TRUE, since it's the only results that I can see or understand. But why work with tainted calculations, when all I have to do is stop what I'm doing, and let it be – and those are the results that always have the deepest meaning: the ones where I can just naturally let go of my personal view and simply let it be. No matter what that "BE" might be. Once I let go – everything becomes clear. I hope that can become part of me without having to remember that it should be part of me; when you have to remember, it means it's not part of who you just naturally are. Remembering is like having to find the key to the door that should already be open. I definitely have to stop locking my doors. Then again, once a door is opened, especially those that are locked, there's never a need for a key again. Certain doors are open for everyone: one plus one is two. No key needed for that. But the doors that cross over into the realm of one plus one may NOT be two, well those are the keys that take a lot of work to find. And the first person to figure out why it's two, or *why it's not two*: well that's the genius.

I guess I'm still figuring out my own genius – I mean, we're all geniuses – even Einstein knew that one. Wow - "even Einstein knew that one"… of course he would know that one – he's a freaking genius! But even a genius among genius' can still be foolish. And not the kind of foolish where you're actually a genius wearing a fool's clothing just to understand someone else's level of genius, or level of foolishness. I'm talking about how Einstein, a genius among genius' - where those very same genius' that HE'S among, are genius' among genius': basically genius to the third. But even that level of genius may not know that one plus one is two, or not two. Simplicity is the hardest task to genius; it goes back to doing nothing, where nothing is always the simplest form. Then again E=MC2 is pretty god damn simple, and has the most meaning in this modern society — so I guess Einstein is really *genius to the fourth*. Who knows what I am — but I do know that KENDRA is only smart. And I don't want smart, I want genius, so it's good that we're not together. I mean, you have to be smart to go to Yale and graduate with honors. She's also an engineer, so there is a practical aspect to her level, which borders on her reaching intelligent, but when you just read books and only understand everything within those books: smart. It's only when you take that same book and apply it elsewhere that you've now reached what intelligence is. And where does genius fall into all of this? A genius writes the book! It's that simple. I knew a genius wrote the book when I heard the first level of genius even involved a book, it's so clear to me — but yet not clear to you. Why? Why was nothing I did ever clear to you? I might not have said *I loved you*, but could you not FEEL that *I loved you* — love is a feeling, not a word; we always have to give words to our feelings to make them mean what we say which is only saying what we feel: but if you can feel without words, and have a meaning based on those feelings which have no words, then you've begun to reach the path of enlightenment. And if you can actually have that path shared with someone else — well

JESUS CHRIST, isn't that THE ONE!? But I guess you're NOT THE ONE, because clearly you didn't see this path that is so clearly a path, that even the most clouded girls could see the sun breaking through to bring clarity to a path that might look clouded only because YOU YOURSELF ARE CLOUDED. God you were so freaking clouded – I mean, who the hell does drugs right in front of someone who doesn't do drugs? Tell me, please tell me – I'm asking? I mean that was such a surreal moment, "I do it because I get cramps" BULL-FUCKING-SHIT, you do it because you're a hippie chick thinking she knows what the fuck it's all about yet knows nothing since every single discovery you had was under the impression of some type of drug. Coffee is a drug – Alcohol is a drug – Marijuana is a fucking drug – Mushrooms – Ecstasy – Acid – DMT – they're ALL FUCKING DRUGS. And what does a drug do: It alters reality! And seeing true reality is the only path to true genius. Yes of course people like Francis Crick can discover DNA and all sorts of crazy shit while under the influence, but fuck all that – they're cheating! Don't they know that? They have to know that! And here's how naïve I was: I still loved you while you took your drugs. I still loved you when I heard the stories of you taking your drugs, and the discoveries you had – and I genuinely was interested in everything you had to say – because in those moments I had no judgments, I had no thoughts – I only felt. My heart was filled every moment we had together. I never judged your past or your present: I do now of course, it's the only way I can actually start over, if you can even call me taking a drive in LA to clear my mind in order to start over, actually starting over, and just now realizing it's only taking me further down the rabbit's whole. But at least I know I need to start over – most people don't, they just keep trying to win the game with only one life left; *it's all about the reset button.*

But then again, I've never been this far in the game – so deep in fact, where I could literally give two shits if I live or die. You know what…? Fuck all of this and fuck her! Here I go talking about dying… AGAIN! And the worst part: it's not even HER DYING… It's my own death I'm contemplating… And since I know I won't die naturally; when life is shitty beyond all fucking measurements of shit - you'll never die in those moments, it's life's crazy-ironic-twisted sense of fucked up humor. But here I am, wishing I was dead! Why? Because some stupid-fucking-hippie-chick made me sad… FUCK HER! She's not even that great. She wasn't that great of an engineer, she wasn't that great of an artist, and she especially isn't that great of a person!

You know how I know you're not a good person: All I can think about when I actually think about you is smashing your fucking face with a hammer! I feel like that would be the only way to put some sense into you – making that pretty little face SINK blow after blow! And for whatever reasons, a hammer is the only tool I can imagine destroying it with. Not the classiest of weapons, but for serving its purpose, it definitely would serve its purpose. Unfortunately, I don't have a hammer.

It's all good though, I can see a Ralph's coming up on the right… and most are open until midnight. I really should buy a hammer right now. But just for fun, and it's only an experiment on the human condition, I want to buy this hammer not with its intended purpose for nails into wood, no-no-no, for this, I want a new reason in mind: smash her fucking face open! I'm not going to actually do it - I just want to see what it feels like to buy a hammer with that purpose in mind. I mean, I don't even kill spiders, so I know its fine that I buy this hammer, and at the end of the day - NO!!! You see, I'm already psyching myself out of this: for this little game, there's only one reason to buy this hammer – SMASH HER FUCKING EYES IN! Fucking hammer, DEEP into her skull! Over and over again until her face is this fucking pile of soft-broken-red bone mush – YES! Okay … It's time to buy a fucking hammer!

# Amstel

Within a grocery store, midnight fast approaching, two checkers talk amongst themselves. The entrance of a man, *eyes filled with intent*, goes unnoticed. The man himself is trapped. Locked away in his own mind, eyes glued to the floor, each step creating the rhythmic beat needed to continue his trance.

Interestingly enough, NEW BEGINNINGS are always the result of a previous end to something. It sounds simple, but the complexity that goes into the NEW *new*, must somehow be related to that which ended, therefore never actually creating something new, just linking a new link into a chain that really has no beginning or end. But what does that actually mean though? Especially for me right now? I mean, here I am looking for the utilities section in a grocery store that I probably shouldn't even be at in the first place. And yet, here I am, unable to determine whether this is the end link to my new beginning, or the beginning link to something that has ALREADY ENDED, or will in fact end. So often we take for granted of where we are, and just accept the fact that where we are, is in actuality, where in fact we're supposed to be. But without the questions of life answered, how can we ever actually know, where in fact we're actually supposed to be. It can all be so confusing at times. The problem is when the focus becomes so drawn to where you are, while you are actually experiencing where you are, hence creating these questions of life: who what when where why and how. The issue I think I'm having is that this is the first time I'm actually understanding this… Right now, within this grocery store; I was beginning to understand this on my way to the grocery store, still driving on Wilshire, but it's not until this very moment that my mind has come up with this conclusion.

But what is the conclusion of all of that?

He begins to zig-zag along the faded black tiles of the store; a diamond pattern, set against the dingy beige floor. Each step perfectly centered within the borders of the square, never stepping on a crack and following it like the yellow brick road. He puts his arms out for balance, as if carefully walking along the tightest of tight ropes. In his mind, the tiles begin to *transform* into a slender, stone-towering-bridge, thousands of miles above the sun; where stars and galaxies explode with light, creating an ever-changing backdrop of mystical colors. Supernovas burst into pulsating-quasars, releasing gases rich in hydrogen and oxygen, the birthing place of light. In the distance, a brilliant blue star burns, encompassed by dancing white flames. The flames join together creating a burning ball of pure energy, timelessly sitting in the eternal void of space. Amstel becomes fixated on the blue star, only furthering his imaginary sequence. Slowly, neighboring planets cross its path – creating circular shadows on the burning blue surface that Amstel must *really look to see*. Each planet no bigger than his own fingernail, where beams of light overshadow his thumb, which is now raised in the sky, blocking one of the planets which he moves with the same timing. He slowly removes his thumb, allowing himself to see the purple planet; its edge brightly glowing pink. There's a mist growing around the planet, an atmosphere of protecting haze, which seems to trap light from escaping back into the eternal void.

High in the sky and not a care in the world – he finally looks down from his stone-laid bridge: A continuous breathing bedrock of molten lava churns. The bubbling top layer of the sun bursts with energy, recycling the fire deep within its core, while simultaneously releasing it back as light. Amstel, as if really on this sun towering bridge, begins to jokingly panic – his arms begin to make giant waving circles, as if trying to maintain his balance, which he finally regains and continues along his imaginary bridge; a childish smirk plastered upon his face.

A break in the diamond formation, creates a pause for Amstel, as he looks to the next sequence of tiles, some four or five feet away. Looking around the store to gage if the coast is clear, he sees the security guard staring back at him, as if anticipating the great and wondrous leap he is about to take. He smiles nervously to the guard, embarrassed to be caught in such a childish act – he regains control, and continues on his search.

*He begins looking up, seeing each sign* and its description of what can be found in the aisle. Beginning on aisle one and slowly moving through the store, he reads 'utilities' on aisle seven and decides to venture through. He passes a lady in her forties, wearing a simple night gown, hair filled with curlers. A box of Lucky Charms sits nicely on top of her cart. Instantly, Amstel's thoughts become visual once again:

> A tiny green leprechaun, prancing through the tall yellow reeds, stumbles upon an old rotting log. The sky is turquoise blue, the clouds are cotton white, and at the base of the log extends the most beautiful rainbow – exploding with color and sparkling with the faintest pin pricks of pure white light. Next to the log sits an old black pot, with a thin wired handle, waiting to be grabbed. The leprechaun, who is tired and exhausted, has traveled for five hundred years in search of his gold. He finally takes his rest, sitting upon the log and pulls out his embroidered handkerchief, where his initials A.J. are inscribed. Wiping the sweat from his forehead, he *slowly begins to take it all in*:

> > A purple-blue butterfly flapping its yellow spotted wings. A crimson red rose releases the sweetest scented pheromones. Long blades of the greenest green grass, while scattered buzzing bumble bees yonder through present-future-past. Golden streaks of yellow lit sun rays, piercing the clouds with a distant smell of rain, while sounds of children laugh with the innocence of youth.

A baby bird chirps, waiting for its mother's food.

A magical blue blanket, which echoes of water sounds, is the spot that was chosen for our green prince to lay down. He's tired and exhausted from a life filled with travel, wanting nothing more than to hear the brook's babble. While his eyes slowly close, and his mind begins to settle, his thoughts become merged with the gold and its kettle.

In the blink of an eye, a man then enters - tall, dressed in black and heartless in his center. In one hand a hammer, the other hand a closed grip, his face twisted, like the devil himself makes him sick. His eyes are blood red, and his hair is ripped out, he slowly looks around, trying to see what it's about. Nothing to him is speaking of beauty, he's only been tortured for all of eternity.

Again and again, he SMASHES the prince's head, until hammer in hand is soaked with red. The leprechaun looks up, to beg and plead, but it will do him no good, it's time to bleed. With hammer in hand and a final smash to the head, the tiny green leprechaun is lifeless and dead.

The man kicks the pot of gold while laughing and dancing, now it is he who has begun his prancing. Wild and free the man dances with glee, grabbing the yondering buzzing bumble bees. Holding them close then crushing with force, he disrupts the very flow of the effervescent rainbow. Eyes still glowing and with the most devilish grin, he rips off the tiny green leprechaun's head. Blood dripping down to the base of its chin, he puts it on a platter and serves it to little kids!

Lost in aisle seven, Amstel becomes locked in a state of nothingness; not even the flicker of an eyelash. He begins to look around the store, breaking his trance and regaining control of his surroundings. He sees nobody, the lady in her forties is already checking out, leaving Amstel alone where he only has his thoughts:

> The issue I think I'm having, is that I've now begun to focus on something with so much focus that although it's becoming an entirely different picture, more clear than the previous, less focused picture, everything else is still revolving around the previous, less focused picture.

> And what kind of life is that? It's like, eventually you'll get to a point where although you've gained new clarity on your surroundings, you remove yourself so far from the grand scheme of things that all that is left is a tiny pixel of what really is the entire world. And even that very pixel will eventually become pixelated – *I mean, where's the end to your thoughts?* What kind of life is this?

The hammer of Thor wouldn't satisfy his urge to find the perfect hammer. But aisle seven, middle shelf and with a

*Penny Saver Coupon, only $3.99* – he became satisfied. He begins to hold the hammer in his hand, letting the handle mold into its most comfortable position, and slowly raising it toward the heavens.

A childhood memory of He-Man suddenly bursts into his mind. He stands there, holding the hammer like the Sword of Power, his snarling tiger sitting strongly by his side. The lights of the store begin to flash, creating a rainbow sequence of sporadic-strobe effects: red glowing beams change to blue neon triangles, twisting themselves into the solid green circles which overlap each other, creating multilayered patterns – each light becoming intently focused on the hammer, giving it a glowing aura of ever-changing radiance. Amstel stands in aisle seven like a pirate; one arm bowed on his waist, the other with his metamorphosing hammer-sword still raised high.

At this point it's become too much for the security guard, who is comfortably leaning against one of the check stands, a toothpick slightly sticking out. He's been watching Amstel ever since his zig-zagging-tightrope-walk, wondering how a grown man can behave in such a way. He begins to calmly walk toward Amstel, who is still standing strong in the middle of the aisle, head tilted upward; with a very large, tooth-showing smile smeared upon his face. As he walks toward Amstel, he begins to look into his eyes – which are hypnotically fixated on the hammer – the guard thinks, at least he seems happy.

Amstel doesn't even notice the security guard, who is now standing by his side.

He quickly jumps, almost dropping the hammer on the ground, "Oh wow… So sorry!" He looks to the guard, "You must think I'm weird or something ---"

He thinks for a bit and then continues, "I'm not though…………

Well okay, I am a little weird, but WE'RE ALL a little weird. It's just that some of us are better at covering it up than others. Like my friend Matt – Dude, this guy is weird! Didn't mean to call you dude… but I mean, he's weird!!!

I mean, this guy can just go up to anybody *in the middle of a grocery store* and like, be normal and stuff…… Yea… Sorry……… I can't do that!"

He remembers himself trying to talk with a woman in produce several years back, "Not at all actually! And believe me… I really do try! I mean, if you think about it, I'm trying right now. BUT… before you say what you're going to say, because I know what you're going to say, I'm not trying in the sense where someone like you would be like, *oh hey stop trying so hard and be yourself*…… no – because that's not what I'm doing!

Because what I'm actually doing, is that I'm trying in the sense NOT to be myself – because if I actually was myself, which don't get me wrong, I would love it everyone was themselves, *but I know you're not* because that's really weird.

But I'm not weird in the sense where I think it's weird to be yourself, I'm weird in the sense where I wish you WOULD BE WEIRD and actually be yourself. *But I know you're not* – because who wants to be weird? I don't...... Even though I am.

But let me ask though, is it weird to say you're weird? Or does the double negative connation of being weird and claiming it, cancel out the weirdness – or is it only like, adding to the weirdness?

You know, like negative one plus negative one is still *negative two.*"

He thinks of the simple math, then continues, knowing he found the next part to it, "Yet... if we *multiply them together* – BOOM, just like that ............ *Positive!*

So now we ask *how*...... How do we, and *by we, I mean you and I; by we, I mean EVERYONE*, become positive off of our negative weird innateness? Granted that you actually follow what I'm saying right now and don't think of my weird as a truly negative weird, I would say all we have to do isssssss???" He looks to the guard, trying to get an answer from him – the guard remains silent, and Amstel continues.

"BOTH be weird!!! And you see just like that, we get to venture to the *positive side of life...* The side with beauty the side with love and fully experiencing EVERYTHING at the absolute, weirdest-high-level……

Then, and really… *only then do we become a positive two*."

The guard checks his watch while scratching the back of his neck, *uninterested* in Amstel's voiced thoughts. Finally the guard looks to Amstel, who is patiently waiting for *something* from the guard, but the guard simply stares back with an empty expression, until finally opening his mouth.

"We're closed now sir – you're gonna have to leave."

Amstel nods his head, *understanding exactly* what being closed is all about.

* * *

Amstel looks to the passenger seat, visualizing the hammer that SHOULD BE, yet isn't. It's begun to rain outside, each street light creating a unique glow, its specific impression on the surroundings. The shrubbery of a tree, darkened to pure shadow - with no details or lines to exemplify its aliveness, becomes lost among the row of trees that line the street. Tiny droplets of water splatter, creating glistening bubbles of light, which stream quickly across all windows. Windshield wipers continually move back and forth, producing hypnotic sounds of nothingness and visually erasing each bubbled universe with every swipe. With every red light, thoughts of going home take over, but *red changes to green* and Amstel continues on his way. Never really knowing what to think or how to feel, or even knowing where he's driving to, yet still knowing he needs to drive.

At the next red light, the next stop, a homeless man is taking cover under the awning of a 7-11. Amstel continues his gaze, wondering the HOW behind his story, but only able to come up with typical stories – the ones we've all heard. He stops his mind from thinking typically by simply observing his surroundings. It's cold and wet outside. The pain this man feels is far beyond Amstel's own realm of pain and suffering. He makes sure no cars are coming, and quickly darts into the convenient store parking lot, where the man is lying down. The homeless man, who seems passed out at the front entrance, doesn't even notice his arrival. The lights of Amstel's car shine directly into the face of the man, who simply pulls his tattered hood over; hiding his face - covering his eyes. Amstel turns his lights out, trying to appease the homeless man's senses. He looks up at his dashboard, which usually has some change and begins to grab it, but then suddenly stops.

> What is this change going to do? I mean really, what, I give the man some change and then I'm suddenly supposed to feel good, or make HIM feel good. If anything, it's almost a slap in the face.

> Maybe it's not about feeling good - Maybe It's about understanding the very reason he's even here. It takes time to understand the reasons for things when you're creating a new reason for something, and have no idea what that reason is, *because you yourself are still in the moment of creation!* What's important now

is to JUST DO - the reasons always come after the doing! Change is only a slap in the face, if you think the change is meant for YOU. But you're giving the change to someone else, therefore, it's not a slap in the face and *more importantly it's not about you.* Every bit of change helps. And if you still think it's a slap in the face – well hey, maybe he needs a slap in the face!

Amstel gets out of his car, covering his head with the top of his own jacket and quickly opens up the back door, pulling out an *umbrella* he keeps in the back seat. Quickly and while still pouring, he runs over to the homeless man, who is now aware of his arrival.

"Here you go." Amstel says, while handing the umbrella to him while thinking how much better than change this is.

The homeless man is genuinely surprised with the random act of kindness, holding up the umbrella in different frames of light, *seeing it for the very first time*:

A simple black umbrella, closed by a strap which encompasses each fold, securely remains closed. The handle, which loops upward, resembles a simple "J" feeling comfortable in the hand. The homeless man, after a careful inspection, slowly begins to unsnap the strap - finding the inner groove, which allows for the umbrella to become open. He opens the umbrella, which is filled with an inner circuit of wires and interlocking metal that bend straight, allowing the umbrella to *stay open*. The man places the umbrella under his own head, looking upward to see the inner mechanics that allow for a complete coverage. He looks to Amstel and smiles, then back to the inner workings of the umbrella. After a few moments, he finally closes the umbrella, and places it by his side.

"Wow…… Thanks brother!" the homeless man excitedly says.

"No problem." Amstel replies, already turning around, feeling the act was finished.

"Wait!" The homeless man shouts, catching the attention of Amstel, "Why are you leaving? Talk with me for a bit."

Amstel looks to the homeless man, sitting there in his own filth, completely covered in dirt and excrement. His blue jeans no longer blue – his red shirt now faded to orange - black Adidas with only one stripe remaining – this is a man whose very smell repulsed the other homeless men from even breaking bread with him. Smells of park bathrooms: stainless steel toilets, connected to wet concrete floors, with no soap to wash or towel to dry. He was a lonely man.

Amstel is uncomfortable furthering the moment with him – he really only wanted to help with the umbrella – talking with the homeless man *adds another dynamic* he's simply not used to. Amstel is thinking about his options, standing over the homeless man, avoiding eye contact while searching within for his answer. The homeless man can of course observe, and understands the thought process going through Amstel's mind – it wouldn't be the first time he's interpreted these types of thoughts from others before. The homeless man crudely waves his arm to Amstel, in a motion to leave.

> "Just go!" he mutters with sounds of desperation, "I mean really…… What's the point, just go!" he looks to Amstel with his deepest expression, "*Nobody is different than nobody else! Just go!*"

The homeless man retreats back into his tattered hooded cave, placing his arms around his knees and slowly putting his head in between. He simply sits there, back in his world, where only he and himself live. Amstel thinks on his next move – *it would be very easy to just leave*; the homeless man has his umbrella, which will at least keep him dry – but it seems a little more complicated than that.

> "And I agree with you," Amstel says, trying to re-spark the conversation, "There really isn't any difference between anybody else."

The homeless man, still covered from the hood of his oversized rain coat, doesn't even acknowledge the attempt. Amstel just stands there, waiting for a response that may or may not come. He looks around the parking lot, mystified by the lights and rain. He looks up to the awning keeping the both of them dry: a steady stream of water continually pours from the top, splashing his shoes from the impact on the ground. He looks to the stream, starting at its highest, and trying to follow that point down to the bottom, as fast as the water falls. He stands there attempting this several times, until finally, his neck begins to hurt; from *jolting back and forth so rapidly*. He looks back to the homeless man, still in his pouty phase.

"Look – I'm really sorry I offended you by thinking about whether or not I should even talk with you – but you can't take that kind of stuff personally. It's not always about you."

Instantly and aggressively, the homeless man throws his arms up, removing his hood and staring coldly to Amstel in the depths of his eyes, "YEA? And it's not always about YOU!" he then, as if in reverse motion, quickly and aggressively throws his hood back on – instantly reverting back to his inverted closed state, arms around his knees, head buried within.

The homeless man refuses to move, locked away in his own thoughts, his mind tucked deep within the boundaries of his own soul. Amstel shakes his head, suddenly not knowing where to place his own arms, but then looks through the store window: an assortment of convenient store foods surrounds him. He becomes captivated by the hodge-podge of goodies, taking one last look at the homeless man, then finally surrendering to his primal urge. He opens the door to the late night shop, the simple entrance beep ringing deep within his mind, which he follows far beyond the boundaries of sound itself - into the depths of vibration - where only waves exist. He sees the wave of sound to the entrance door, slowly begin to stretch itself into a single solid line, which then turns in toward itself, creating a perfect circle. The pulsating circle shrinks in size, allowing it to fit in the hand, where there it rests. *He focuses on the circle in the palm of his hand,* becoming entranced by the imagery, yet never losing the purity of the sound wave itself – still ringing within his ears.

"Sir?" the clerk asks, "do you want that doughnut?"

Amstel looks up, at a loss for words, "I don't know." He looks to the clerk, "To be honest I didn't even know it was a doughnut until you just said so." He begins to look back at the sprinkle covered doughnut, sitting in the palm of his hand, once again becoming captivated; this time of course, not through the sound vibration.

"Yea the pink ones my favorite!" the clerk adds, smiling like an infant, "It's like, SO GOOD!"

Amstel looks back to the clerk, seeing an awkwardly social, thick-framed glasses wearer, smiling to Amstel as if the doughnut really was SO GOOD. His smile, mostly covered by braces and patches of yellow, which somehow blended into the braces, was genuine. Amstel smiles back as genuinely as he can, the freckles on the clerks face masked by a thin layer of acne, which somehow also blended into each other.

"Yea maybe on the way out," Amstel says, "I think I want to have a look around first." He smiles again to the clerk, who begins to blow his nose on an old tissue, which was lodged in his pant pocket. Amstel just nods, still watching the clerk observantly, then finally turns around.

An entire world of desire, placed within the tiny con-founds of a late night shop, resonates with different fre-quencies. Each related to a specific desire that is intended when entering the store. Hence the initial sound vibration, which transformed into the very doughnut, that brought him in to hear the sound that transformed into the dough-nut in the first place. Every part, fitting together to form an overall function, allowing desires to be realized. This is the essence of the late night shop – which fully captivates Amstel. Slowly and patiently understanding each com-ponent, within the walls that create the very component, allowing Amstel a *clarity never achieved before*:

> Cheesy puffs ARE toothpaste and toothpaste ARE cheesy puffs – they just arrive at they're form at dif-ferent times within our lives – like an *almost* infinite elemental half-life, since time itself IS infinite – then anything that is not truly infinite in its own nature has it's very own half-life, changing into new pieces particles and *parts* – these P's might last for almost an eternity, like the bag of cheesy puffs, but eventually, it will break down into a different P, allowing that possibility to exist, and remembering that time is infinite, it can then become, over an almost infinite amount of time, tooth-paste. Wow!

> I don't know what to make of that.

He continues his move through the aisle – focusing his attention on anything and everything within his myopic spectral view of overall true vision. Until finally, his heart begins to race uncontrollably, losing all thoughts and sense of reason. Blood begins to flow throughout his body, creating a sensational warmth that begins to entice his nerves to fire hysterically, creating sporadic shaking within his hands and fingers. His eyes become dilated, sweat begins to race from his forehead, and feelings of nausea and excitement join together creating super feelings of power and confusion. There in front of his eyes: a simple hammer, waiting to be grabbed.

$$* * *$$

An infinite stretch of highway, dampened by continuous rain, catches and holds each speck of light; where blurred patches of color transcend into beams, breaking through the flatness of the infinite grid, presenting itself as an ever changing cycle of pathways; infinite in nature, yet only visible at certain angles and degrees.

Right turns and lefts become sudden glimpses of roads not taken; *transportations never understood.* Continuing straight on the pathway of destruction, Amstel finds himself unable to decipher the deeper messages every instant can hold. From the lonely man standing on the overpass, to the happy family, laughing and singing in the car next to him. Each of these moments becomes part of the infinite stretch that within the mind of Amstel, are unchanging now and *negatively* set in stone.

> Understanding the concept of time as a loop, rather the Mobius strip, can be problematic if you feel you're not even living on the strip. It's like, okay I know I'm supposed to be going this way – forward through

time – always moving forward - but I can't help but to stop and really try to understand the inner workings of the strip itself: simply taking the necessary time of reflection on how I even made it this far in the first place. Of course, the very action of this reflection – the pause in moving forward - obviously disrupts the flow of what is needed to be, a continually moving forward constant. So now what am I supposed to do? It seems I've literally destroyed any hope of EVER getting back to any neutral timing in life. Everything is now negatively set because of one simple miscalculation in life. And the crazy thing is, it didn't even seem to be that big of a deal when it was actually happening – just another moment of something that did NOT want to work itself out; which I was always able to understand. But then why after this, did everything go SO FUCKING BADLY? So badly in fact that I'm now on my way to destroy the *very cause* that has brought me to a point of understanding the *true effect* of what this cause was actually able to create in terms of an actual effect – this is even more crazy since now the effect of course is making me destroy that *very cause*, to that which created the *true effect* in the first place. I'm pretty sure in time machine lingo, I would be erasing my own existence with this act – which I guess is the idea: to somehow reset my timing in whatever dimension or universe it needs to be reset to, where I can then become timed BACK on the Mobius strip – unaware of my own miscalculations of any mistimed mistake.

I think this is just *way too much for you in the lower sense…* I mean – you have no variation in your life. No UP, everything is just down! Even the Mobius strip has a twist – it's the only way it can actually function. But really though – why would you ever base a decision when you're working from below ground zero? When you're this low – there really is no way to get back up, at least not naturally. You really need to do something that is just unexpected, that then can begin to reset the natural flow of timing.

Amstel is finally at Kendra's place – who lived on the sidewalk pathways of the Venice beach canal system; overgrown with giant eucalyptus trees, which are interwoven by stringing lights, creating a glowing ambiance of calming subtlety. Each home with a unique theme, yet somehow connected to a larger scale of interdependence, based on the house to its left and right. This interconnectedness creating the specific vibe of communal family – going beyond the typical hello and tapping into the truth - each member living within this framework provides.

*Kendra was only a visitor:* moving from the east coast several years prior and finding an empty guesthouse along the pathway, gave her a *limited access* to this community. It was the look she provided that allowed for her acceptance here, blending into the array of designer-hippie-hipsters, showing more on the outside than within.

Nonetheless, the home she stayed in was beautiful. Simple and elegant, with a lined fence, covered by vines and overgrown shrubbery. Upon entrance, perfectly trimmed half-sized pine trees, twist and turn, fighting for limited sun which occasionally breaks through the larger trees, still occupying most of the space. A Zen style coy pond, covered by a maple bridge, creates a temperament of peace. Several benches, placed sporadically yet with precision, sit nicely upon perfectly trimmed grass; lime green in nature. It was a calming house – soothing in every way possible – except for the *guest* who lived inside.

Amstel turns his engine off, peering through the shrubbery of the overgrown fence. A distant light peeks through the branches, creating flickering silhouettes that move back and forth, like the purple planet, crossing the path of its burning blue sun – someone is home.

Amstel looks to the hammer, sitting comfortably on the passenger seat and slowly reaches for it. He holds the hammer, letting the handle fit the inner contours of his own hand once again – The He-Man strobe effects vanished from his mind. A tight grip begins to loosen, then becomes tight again, feeling the different weights each hold has. A cycle of inconsistency begins to flood his mind, as the moment of truth draws upon him.

> I really have no idea what to do right now! I don't even think I have any more thoughts to think of – everything to think on this matter has already been thought out – which simply leaves me with this empty conclusion. But I guess that's the difference between action and the IDEA of action: once the actual action is supposed to take over, there are no

more ideas that can flow from it. I've now reached that point.

He continues to sit in the car, holding the hammer and feeling its weight. Occasionally, looking out his window, which is still covered by beads of water. He moves closely to the window, his nose touching the glass, staring through a single bead, curving the nature of light; temporarily distracting him from the decision that must be made. His entire vision, bending to the flow that twists his entire perception, creating a new world where the old laws don't apply. He's captivated by the curvature – thinking of Einstein and his laws that unfolded – reminded of MC Escher and his self-portrait within the bubble – each brilliant mind creating a separate meaning from the very thing he was peering into. Was there not pain associated with these lives? Hidden truths discovered through the *catalyst of pain*. Van Gogh chopped his own ear off – and so many others of society who have felt the pain that Amstel himself was dealing with. Is it not part of the human condition to be vulnerable and simply not know the reasons for the pain each of us feels? He begins to look at his own life, trying to understand the things he has done – the positive things that transcend his own being and somehow have touched others. He cannot think of any. Nothing to show for his life – nothing to claim as his own doing, or the *helping to those who then create their own doing*. Although he is empty inside, is that not the necessary condition to then become filled? Although he is now void of coherent thoughts to categorize exactly what he is going through, he does have feelings and feeling never lie. He knows he genuinely does not want to destroy. All he's ever wanted, and it's what everyone truly wants – is to be loved.

*The simple idea of love*; where true parity within is equally joined at the highest level. A level that Amstel, in his current lower state, cannot conceive. Even within the depths of his own mind a truth is apparent: low level ideology only receives low level input – within this lower level everything becomes tainted – from simple water molecules freezing and no longer becoming fluid in nature – to he himself, caught in the trenches of thought, creating only havoc and pain within his own fibers of being. His deepest self is right – something must change within him, and it will not come from that of a hammer or any other pain he wishes to inflect on himself or others. Although he is unaware of the actual remedy for his problems, the band aid and cure-all for his pain – he is still a child, lost in a world of darkness and heartache. He begins to see his child self, a distant memory slowly unfolds:

A giant circus tent stands before his eyes, where strings of multi-colored flags dangle and dance around the solid wooden poles lining the tent. Amstel is young, only five or six, holding a red balloon in one hand, with an ice cream cone in the other. Within a moment, the ice cream falls and the balloon begins to fly away, creating a simple cause and effect, that at the time he cannot understand or comprehend. He begins to cry and wail – screaming in discomfort over a lost balloon and ice cream cone. His mother, like most mothers, naturally helps heal his pain by her warming comfort. Within a few moments, the pain of losing the balloon and ice cream are the past – and he continues on the path of his circus day: lions tigers and bears.

Is he not now experiencing another cause that creates a similar effect to that of his lost balloon and ice cream cone? The pain throughout these moments, although different causes – still create similar effects. Effects of pain – loss – desire for something that is just no longer possible to have. *If it was to be had – it would be had.*

The sudden flood of input to Amstel's mind is overwhelming – he begins to cry, throwing the hammer on the floor, and buckling his arms to hide his face. Sobbing uncontrollably - disgusted and ashamed for how far he travelled down – the only place left for comfort, the only place for escape, is back home… to his mother.

* * *

Amstel drives for several hours through the depths of an autumn's night; the majority of leaves already scattered upon the ground, finding their final resting place within the gutters and sewers that are brimmed with bottom dwellers. Very few leaves remain perched high among the branches, waiting for their final breeze to come crashing down, hoping to find a spiraling path that catches the eye of a beholder – serving a final purpose of beauty.

Amstel arrives to his childhood home at around 5:30 in the morning. The desert moon, still over powering the morning light, which is beginning to break through the sky. His mother's home is a typical suburban desert house;

sandy rock based ground with cacti sporadically growing, towering over the sphered desert bushes which are prickly in nature and *green in color*. Each bush trimmed to perfection by the Mexican gardener who visits his mother twice a week. At the center of the front landscaping, a single Acacia tree stands alone, lined by white bricks that create the perfect circle to encompass the tree. Within the circle, only a few weeds have the strength to over-power the rocks, poking their heads out and basking in the morning dew. Each weed special in nature – wild and free in spirit – and only growing where flowers dare not.

His mother finally found her peace in the dessert – although living alone for most of her adult life, it wasn't until her move to the tranquil nights of the desert, that she found her personal acceptance of who she is and what she was. What she was, Amstel only had a glimpse: the lost photo within the box of photos: his mother in a bikini, two handsome men by her side, sitting around a bon fire with guitar in her hands. The stories of Woodstock: only told with a filter, but enough said to allow Amstel to understand his mother was much different than he.

But he truly loved his mother – although it was seldom that he found himself visiting – he still considered her part of his life, even though to most, his relationship seemed distant. But distance is always based on perspective, and within Amstel's own perspective – his mother was his best friend – and at times, she was his only friend.

Slowly and carefully he opens the screen door, trying not to wake his mother, who he hasn't seen in four or five years.

The security light quickly shines upon his face, which he covers with his hand and begins to crack the door open – peeking with his head to make sure the coast is clear. The TV is still on, emitting an ambient glow throughout the living room, ever changing with colors and shadows. He begins the arduous tip-toe to his bedroom, which surprisingly, his mother kept up all these years. Crossing the path of the TV, he disrupts the light shadows displaced among the living room, much like the planet of the blue star. A very tired voice calls out.

"Amstel?"

He looks toward the voice, which is sourced from the living room, and whispers back, "oh … hey mom." Still blocking the light from the TV, allowing his mother to see her son's shadow, which is framed with light.

"Is everything alright… What time is it?" His mother confusedly asks.

"Everything's fine mom," he calmly says. "We can talk in the morning." He quickly goes to his room, and shuts the door. *Compelled to lock it – yet having the wisdom to resist.* What seems like the very next instant: his mother is already sitting at the edge of his bed, staring deeply at the son she hasn't seen, to what her, felt like an eternity.

He looks to his mother, who now seems glowing from the desk lamp, giving the room its radiance. She seems heavenly in sprit, an aura, which is too much for him. He looks away from his mother, the shadows of her body becoming transcribed on the wall, making her much bigger than she really is. He begins to fixate on the shadow images, seeing his mother's darkness for the very first time: she's a troll – sitting under a bridge, hunched over, waiting for information to feed her starving, mal-nourished soul. The shadow lacks a neck; no connection between mind and body – just this shadow-blob, put under a bridge to serve one purpose: to feed off others.

He closes his eyes, making everything disappear into the abyss of his deeper self. Only there - comfort arises: the blanket of inner peace begins to take him on a journey through the formation of colors. His vision completely erased from the *protection closed eyes provides*; he sees the checkered, crisscross fabric of true vision begin to unfold. It moves as a wave pattern, originating in the center then slowly moving toward all edges.

As it approaches the edge, it begins to separate, creating multilayered folds that transcend back to the epicenter of creation; only strengthening the very fold that created the unfolding nature of the fold which unfolded to the fold that created the fold to unfold in the first place. He sees the *back and forth* that waves consist of, each back *creating the forth* that allows the wave to move through space and time – each piece – each back no different than it's forth, *just different timing in each cycle.*

Suddenly, his fractaled mind tangles, releasing his self from his deeper self – thoughts begin to flood, breaking the barrier, quickly forcing him to open his eyes; rebalancing the world around him.

* * *

He has breakfast with his mother - the shadows of her troll-self buried deep within his mind – the morning sun now peeking through the rose stitched curtains; a single beam of light extends through the kitchen, hitting the silver-plated sink. Particles of dust dance freely through the golden beam – intertwining their essence with the warmth it provides. The light slowly moving throughout the kitchen, *its reach touching everything with time and patience.* The bacon begins to crackle – the smell dances its way to Amstel, seducing him to the brink of a breaking point.

> "Mom, don't you know I'm vegetarian!?" he abruptly speaks to his mother, "What are you doing eating bacon anyway – it's so unhealthy for you!"

> Without looking up, his mother continues to turn the bacon, "Amstel – I'm sixty-nine years old, if I want to eat bacon… I'm gonna eat bacon!"

> "You're sixty-nine?" He asks confusedly, "I thought you were sixty-seven?"

> Still looking down at the frying pan, she responds, "Sixty-nine Amstel."

> "Are you sure?" he asks, *genuinely thinking she's wrong.*

"Yea I'm pretty sure." She glances to her son, where they have an instant moment of connection:

*Where is the truth?*

I mean if you are going to talk to your mother – at least understand who she is and what her purpose is. She's not here to serve you! Hence her cooking the very bacon she COULDN'T serve to you if she wanted to serve you in the first place. So there is something else to this relationship - that unfortunately, because of the fact that all you can talk about is whether or not she's sixty-seven or sixty-nine – that you're missing right now. *You must understand what truth your mom has for you.* Talk truth to her, and see where SHE leads the conversation – there you will find the absolute truth, since she would never lie to you. She knows far more than you can even comprehend – including how old she is.

"Okay, I don't know about your whole age thing, but I do know when *Jesus* was turning twenty-six, and I gave him his birthday card, he was all, 'dude, why did you write twenty-six… I'm twenty-five *brother*!' And I was like… *Um, no you're not!* And then of course he said… *Um, yea I am!* Then he told me his birthdate, August fifth 1986, which means he's only one year younger than me, so guess who was right? Yours truly. *I mean he actually thought he was,* you know - turning twenty-five, when he was actually turning twenty-six. What's even worse, is that he genuinely lost an entire year of his life – all because of a simple mistiming issue. I gotta say though, it was pretty sad to see his face when he finally figured it all out – it was so realistic too, and of course tragic – I guess most tragedies are realistic."

His mother listens so intently, that it takes her a few seconds to respond, "How is Jesus?" she asks, "You know I've always loved him."

"Yea I know, he's okay - I guess we both thought living with each other was going to be different than it actually is…"

"How so?"

"Eh it's hard to say… I mean, I always knew Jesus did a lot of things to *expand his mind* – but to have it so close to me now, well…… it's just a little off-putting. And of course he's always like, 'dude, you really do need to open up, and expand YOUR mind and you should do this and you should do that and blah blah blah…… I mean, you know my policy on people who say SHOULD a lot - I mean, I'M OPEN! Not as open as him of course, *but that's Jesus for you.*

"Are you taking any drugs?"

"What!?!? Mom!!! Don't ask me that question – I mean really. *Don't ask me that!* First of all, I never like to answer questions that I myself would *never ask.*

And second – you're my mom. So it's already kind of tainted."

His mother puts down the spatula, and looks to her son in disbelief "You think because I'm your mother it's tainted? Wow, Amstel! You really have no idea about anything" She shakes her head and goes back to her bacon.

"I didn't mean it like that……"

His mother, almost throwing the spatula against the stove, "Well how do you mean it then!? What have I ALWAYS told you…? Say what you mean for Christ sakes. *This is your biggest problem – you're just talking to hear yourself talk most of the time!*"

"Okay okay, I mean…………." He thinks deeply for a few seconds, then continues, "Well I don't know what I mean."

"*Then don't speak!*"

Amstel nods, while his mother brings over her breakfast plate of bacon, the golden beam of light still moving throughout the kitchen. Amstel sits there, watching his mother eat bacon, while the dust flies about – in silence they sit.

* * *

Amstel takes his mother to a health food store – where they specialize in juice and smoothies. He sits there, explaining the principles of juicing, and the mind blowing effects it can have on the body. He enlightens her with the story of his own, *all green juice diet;* where he didn't eat for six weeks - and by the end saw with such a clarity, that it actually became clouded again – yet *still clear*. She is very impressed. He explains to her his work, going through the details of how it really just comes down to stealing ideas – in a non-stealing way. She is very impressed. He talks with her about skateboarding – explaining once again, the new style of surf and skate he discovered at Venice Beach, and the people that line the boardwalk, living in a world of mystery – yet not so mysterious. She is very impressed.

As Amstel searches his mind for the next thing he can explain to his mother to impress her, she stops him to ask a question.

"Amstel honey?" he looks to her, "Why did you come home last night?"

She asks with such truth in her voice, that he doesn't know where to begin – she continues for him.

"You know sweetie, in my life, I've had to run home more times than I can even count – and usually it was because of some guy and a broken heart. I mean, I've told you about a few of them, but those are only the ones that I feel comfortable sharing. There's some stories out there that rocked my world SO MUCH, that I couldn't even find myself going home – I just, well........ *kept going.*" She takes a moment to reflect, then continues.

"And isn't that the story we all make for ourselves – the tales of HOW we kept going in whatever circumstance we faced that somehow wanted to stop us from continuing on our journey?"

Amstel nods, encouraging his mother to continue.

"I mean… do you even realize how lucky you are? You're at a point right now where you can do whatever you want! And I really do mean *you can do whatever you want*…… You know eventually, you hit an age where there isn't much more you can do."

He stops her, "Don't talk like that mom, you can always do what you ---"

"Amstel – let me finish…… *This is not about me! I've accepted my life, and because of that – I am truly happy.* But I also had to really push myself at times to keep going – and I think *the hardest times I had, was when going back home just wasn't an option for me.* I mean, you can always come home to me – heck, you can live here if you want – but I think we both know, that's just not who you are – that's not how we move forward. *I think the hardest part of moving forward, is when you no longer see a clear path to move forward on……* But at the same time… that's when it becomes up to you to *create the path* that you actually want to move forward on."

He thinks for a bit, "but *how?*"

*"This one isn't a how question, Amstel — it's when?"*

She waits for him to absorb *the idea of when*, then continues.

"Because *when* is based on timing — and **you create** *what timing is your timing.* Timing isn't something that's random and just happens when it happens. *Timing is the* **meaning** *you associate with time itself.* And since it's the meaning that YOU associate with everything, then it only makes that *everything* is meant to have meaning.

*There is meaning to EVERYTHING… you just have to find it."* She thinks deep for a moment, *"or it finds you."*

* * *

The flat plane of the desert stretches to the horizon — calling out to venture — wherever it may lead. Hours go by; continuing to advance, facing the flat-depthless-abyss. Unaware of where to go, yet knowing the time has come to go — to free the self from the past and venture into the future; where the present moment is the only truth that can be seen or understood.

Something within propels ideas forward *through repetitive nature* - continuing the same thought pattern — creating new streams that follow the flow of the previous flood.

The flood itself – erasing that which is no longer needed – preparing to build something new, withstanding the next flood of knowledge; which is ready to erase that which is no longer needed, creating overlapping circles. Building strong is the key to withstanding the forces of nature. Yet the strength of the ship that's built to resist the flood is dependent on the very propellers that are built within the ship to propel it *through the flood.*

Ships naturally *float* – yet masterly moving forward – that's unnatural. *It's the unnatural aspect to our lives that matter* – only there can we find the progress that allows for our advancement into the natural: the ability to float while moving forward.

One could sail around the world – moving forward here – floating there. Yet throughout this voyage: the *combination of the two* may never find itself.

For this to happen, a simple idea must be *rooted into the seed,* which then creates the very root, which in turn will grow to produce more seeds with their own roots:

*Learn to move forward through floating.*

* * *

He floats his way to the forest. *Never comprehending the exact how* in which he arrives – yet knowing his arrival is met with the aliveness, that only *true-green surroundings* can evoke – hence *removing the questions of how.*

Beautiful rich pine trees, blossoming with pine cones of abundance, tower over one another – allowing enough light to feed the plush ferns that scatter the forest floor. Light breaks through the needles, creating ever-changing shimmers, which electrify colors to *transform* to their full brightness. Darkened damp soil, wet from moisture and cold to the touch – becomes enriched with warmth, as sunrays shed energy, illuminating darkness with light. He places his hands in the cold wet soil, digging as deeply as his fingers will allow, uprooting tiny blades of grass and examining the roots so closely he can smell the earth: so large in size, yet, with the ability to shrink itself into the palm of his hand. He holds the earth close, cupping it like water, and slowly allowing it to drizzle out of his hands – returning it to the source of its creation. He does this several times, looking at the tornado pattern of dirt falling, creating a small mound of lively displaced soil. He buries his hands through the bottom of the mound, feeling the fresh laid dirt sit nicely on top – the sensations of a simple dirt pile brings a large smile to his face.

He looks at his hands - his fingernails now covered with dirt, where granules of grit are wedged deep within the cracks of his very own hard and soft. He looks closely at this line between his finger and fingernail – only created through the dirt that has mapped out the very line he is now focusing on. Without this dirt – without this line, without this map, where would he be looking? He has no idea. But the very idea of creating an idea around something he has no idea about – intrigues him.

He's always had to know the reasons for things, or at least have some grasp on his reality to quantify exactly what he is viewing – but this dirt-created-line within the confounds of his own reality, has done just that – created an actual reality, where he no longer needs any reasons behind what his reality is. His new world is based on whatever he wants to call his own. Sure he could be looking at the trees right now, but in this moment, the reality he has created, is that of his own fingernail. Which for him – is everything! It's the entire world - it's the universe – it's anything he has ever seen, known or thought he could know, simply put into his finger. *His world, his reality, is whatever he wants it to be.*

He walks through the forest – alone and free from the oppression of his thoughts, which had become melded with others. Free from the hauntings of deceitful desires, beautiful flowers begin to blossom, opening their essence and sharing their secrets: the secrets of spirals were always known to him – yet now – they become reality. The spiral itself: the evolutionary step from the second into the third dimension becomes real. He sees a circle within the center of a flower, becoming a three dimensional sphere – yet it is NOT a sphere, it is not a complete three-dimensional object, it's a spiral - no connection between beginning and end; no actual beginning or end, hence the non-connection. Yet this ability to create a link, or a *catalyst* into the third dimension, is *based on its ability to break its previous link* from the second dimension of the circle, into the third dimension of the sphere; or what actually is the universe – which creates its roots in the galaxies that allows for the flower to grow its roots in the first place. Following the same sequence of rules that allow for this existence and creation is the infinite loop that binds us all. We are three dimensional beings, created by two dimensional rules, which only become expressed when broken through from the second dimension, *hence creating a new dimension.*

He allows himself to sit by a creek, thinking about dimensions and watching the rippling water break over rocks, where *time begins to slow.*

Sitting comfortably in the dirt, a single patch of grass catches his attention, he looks away from the water to focus down on the grass; which transforms in front of his eyes – becoming a unique forest, where blades of grass become mountain high trees – a separate world detached from his own, yet connected through his own interpretation of what this new world actually is. *While on his hands and knees*, he understands just how BIG everything is: How big the individual blade of grass and the tiny bugs that compose the ground are and the *components* that create that tiny blade and the bugs. The very nature of nature is becoming clear. He sees himself without seeing himself – he hears the tree fall without hearing the tree fall – his senses become more alive, since his senses are becoming senseless. He is beginning to detach himself from all things, and in a sense – become all things, forming new attachments while creating new beginnings.

He sees only a *glimpse* of all of this – but it's enough to captivate, creating the understanding that there is much more than he can ever comprehend. He focuses back on the grass, the separate world from his, trying to re-vision the forest that had laid before his eyes – it's back to its grass state, the rippling water now overwhelming in sound, enough to re-focus. He begins to look back to the water, until his mind tangles again, creating thoughts and observations that remove him from the water. He starts to walk, the creek resonating in descending sound, the Doppler effect showing itself through water-wave-sounds.

The more he walks, the further the sounds of water and the phantoms of lost loves become his reality. These morbid fantasies of pain were once set in stone – concrete formations that seemed unbreakable - yet the stones do just that; they stay put. *Away from it all, he actually becomes away from it all* – casting his stones into the bottomless well, making countless wishes with every toss.

* * *

After several hours of roaming, he finds his way back to his car – *without searching or wanting* – his car just appeared. The full circle of his hike: only created through the zig zag patterns of his back and forth, combined with the spiraling nature of moving forward, while never moving straight, creates feelings of precision. He is exactly where he's supposed to be. He throws his arms into the air – free once again from the slavery of a prisoned mind – enjoying his rightful place in the universe; *now understanding it as his own.*

It's quite incredible – I mean really really incredible! Sure I've heard stories of people leaving it all behind and finding happiness – but again, that's only what you hear or read – it just goes to an *infinitely higher level once you're the one who's actually leaving it all behind.* I mean sure, I'm only three or four hours away from Los Angeles, but STILL – I'm away from Los Angeles – and the best part – nobody, and I really-do-mean nobody even knows where I am right now. For all they know, I could be in freaking India – sitting under a tree, eating fruit!

Could that be your destination?

He opens his car door, looking around once again, at the inspiring forest that held infinite secrets to reality. He closes his eyes while breathing it all in, simply being his true being, without being at all. He's happy. Happier than he's ever been – alone with only himself, which until he was actually alone with himself, would have seemed crazy – since before, whenever he was alone with his self, his mind still played tricks on him – but now, since his tricks have stayed behind – he finds his ultimate freedom. His ultimate playground of ascending truth: filled with a jungle gym of experiences that only a jungle's gem could create.

As he enters his car – surprisingly a flyer has been placed on his windshield. *He goes to reach it, struggling at first* while trying to stretch over his door - until finally, his fingers grasp the flyer safely bringing it inside. He wonders how a flyer could have gotten there in the first place – he didn't see anybody on his adventure through the forest of third dimension intellect – *yet he accepts, even though he's quite puzzled.* It doesn't matter – the flyer made it, safe and sound. Interestingly enough, he never used to look at flyers on his windshield – they simply found their way to the floor, without ever getting to express what they intended to express. He suddenly thinks of past loves, who also *never got to express what they truly wanted to express,* they just ended up on the floor – until for them, hopefully somebody else comes along, ready to receive their full message – keeping them safe and sound.

He looks at the flyer, *knowing this one will not go to the floor – YOSEMITE NATIONAL PARK.*

* * *

He begins to head north, while driving with the clarity needed to know, the drive is correct. His thoughts continually staying clear – *no longer thinking whether this is right or wrong, just experiencing as much as possible,* without understanding or putting to words exactly what he is comprehending. Before long, he has driven for hours, the landscape changing ever so slightly – yet enough to see that he's entering a new realm. The mountains begin to show them self; giant jagged peaks with rocks melded into the mountainside, where sideway growing trees find enough light to survive and cast their shadows onto the twisted windy road. The slender pass through the California cliffs, block the sun, creating a cold front that forces Amstel to roll up his window. While doing so and simultaneously putting the heat on, he begins to wonder where he will sleep. He has no tent – just his car, and as much warmth as his car would provide, he somehow wants the true wilderness experience – since it's something he has never done.

Yes of course he had gone camping – but not in the sense where his camping would transform itself into his actual home. While daydreaming about whether or not he is ill-prepared and should just go home, at least to get supplies, a Big 5 sporting goods store shows itself – once again, the universe projecting the truth that he is on the right path. He smiles and exits toward the superstore.

He roams the store for twenty minutes, looking at all of the trinkets and gadgets involved with camping. He's reminded of his previous search for a hammer, and how in the timespan of twenty-four hours – *everything has changed.* He finally finds his section – which creates chaos in his mind; through the sheer overabundance of how many tents actually exist. He has no idea on which tent to choose, he just stands there, lost in a new aisle – of a new store – with a new thing to search for. It becomes overwhelming for him – he's not meant to have a tent, this he finally realizes – he leaves and heads for the ocean. Yosemite can wait.

* * *

The beautiful blue, of the blue beautifully blue, beckons to your every whim. Creating *trembles of fear* with each wave rolling in. You suddenly feel through the pores of your skin…

The beautiful dolphin – showing you its fin.

Amstel arrives to an abandoned sand dune, the lighter shades of sand becoming distinctly visible, through the sun's set and the moon's rise. Peaking over the mountain cliffs, the moon's glow touches the face of Amstel; a waxing-crescent with streaks of faded clouds smeared across the evening sky. A collaboration of colors extends, lighting tiny grains of sand, which echo and glow with subtlety. Amstel looks across the deserted beach, the glistening glitter shimmering each flicker to dance and sparkle, becoming captivated by the finite points of light – joining together to engulf his senses. The sand grows from the beach front, wave after wave pounding, forming a new ground to stand upon – *from the water grows the earth*. Each wave brings new – although small in nature, it's the very *speck* of sand that grows the beach.

While still periodically glancing to the moon, which slowly makes its rise into the night sky. Several cars begin to roll in, beginning their task of pitching their tent; each seeming happy to do so. A younger couple is among them, shifting their surfboards to better position the room they have available, smiling to each other in the process.

Amstel is a mere observer, understanding as much as he can, while trying to commit himself to the moment. The couple glances to Amstel, inviting him to come over with their eyes and a smile. Amstel nervously walks toward the couple, but seeing their faces lit with joy transcends, lighting him up as well.

They build a bond fire together – allowing Amstel to witness the bond the fire creates – they talk for hours – lost in the moment everything connects, understanding truths never understood before: Individual truths that only truthful individuals create. *Nothing becomes binded through the purity of spirit.* No boundaries to enforce or borders to protect – it all becomes one, *shared together yet experienced separately*; the sharing nature of sharing becomes part of their nature. Giving while receiving, while dismissing either or, allows for *transcendence into higher realms*, where conversation reaches its peak:

The slowly developed progress where clouds become *new ground*; creating foggy undertones, which confuse proper standing points – allows one to fly, creating the eagle eye – comfortably soaring to new heights, while seeing the mouse who *trembles with fear, afraid* to take that step out of its grounded cave – giving the eagle its ultimate understanding.

Unfortunately for Amstel – he was the mouse; locked away in an eagle's body – waiting for the moment to come; seeing himself for who he is and what he was – waiting for his opportunity to begin his soar into the heights, where seeing his old self scavenging on the ground and trembling with fear *becomes the cause* for the eagle that he is, to take away the mouse that he was – unlocking him to become. *Everything becomes*, creating an endless cycle that connects mouse to eagle, allowing each form to exist simultaneously, yet separate from the previous or here-after form. Mouse is eagle – eagle is mouse. Yet when mouse is mouse it is not eagle it is mouse, when eagle is eagle it is not mouse it is eagle.

Amstel is patient to find that which releases him into his true, soaring through the clouds form – *or **she** will find him, scattering among the ground.*

# Sparks

*What are you writing?* That was the first time I heard that question from the character in my head that wanted me to write about the character in my head – the character in my head that I've been writing about. It wasn't even really a character per say, more of an actual being within my own being that controlled the very being that I was. What's even more interesting about this being, more so than being a completely separate being from my own, is that it took a very long period of time for me to even realize that there even was a being within my own being that would soon become my actual true being. *The character that resides within all.*

It's always a slow progression into the progression of truth. But if you are unaware of certain truths, what then do you progress towards? I think for most in this world, the very idea that you are not you; rather you are a collection of the memories that have collected within you to then be portrayed in a creative manner, ensuring that the *creative you* can then survive – through the works that the creative-you-outlet has created, can be a little daunting.

There's a simple example of this idea though through the very sharing of one's creativity. Any piece of creative outlet:

from a poem written to a photograph captured or even an *essay* – can be viewed as a sort of signature. Not from the body of that individual who captured or wrote the piece in discussion, because body is only skin deep – rather it comes from a place where every generation has given a completely separate name, yet is intertwined with the *very same essence* that can then *spark* the name to come about. I would like to say the first name of this was given to the Sun. The very light that in truth was all light around our world. Yet as light grows to greater understanding, we as a species, break off from the original, to then create *separate parts* from the giant whole. Unfortunately (or fortunately, depending on perspective) the next level of *spark* would arise in God.

Where the very idea of god spread himself out like a virus, no longer staying "God" but then transcending his name through countless generations of creative outlets – cross cultural outlets that spread across the globe *in the form of a name.* The sun became God, which means God became the Sun – God became Zeus – God became Shiva – God became Allah – God became Jesus – God became Buddha, and so on and so on. Everyone knows this – this is nothing new.

The very essence to our humanity, the liveliness of our lives, the ability to understand more than any other spe-cies EVER to walk this earth – the Human Being in us all, first decided NOT to think selfishly with what gives us this power – this breath of life, this vision of beauty, this tran-scending journey into unknown ideas – for early Humans it was a source of unknown ability which seemed to flow through our veins – something was able to take us into new ideas that previous generations were unable to grasp and each of these generations decided to embark on journeys, as a collective whole – into what truly could be discovered. Creating the very generations that lived within those specific times of discovery that created the gaps from the previous generation, allowing for a progression and ascension into a *new generation.*

The Human Being at their core was developed in a higher realm – a level of looking up into the heavens and deciding that there was in fact a heaven to be called. But what is so interesting about this idea: the idea of calling the notion of looking up, heaven, and calling *the spark,* god – is that it was developed THOUSANDS of years ago. Yet from thousands of years ago, simple ideas have held true in the minds of people. People who accept truth without actually ever understanding the HOW behind the truth. Without the understanding of how, everything becomes lost.

Imagine you wake up one day, and you are no longer living where you are so habituated to living all of your life – rather you are in a completely new land - with completely new people, speaking an entirely different language. The landscapes are different, the seasonal change more drastic than previous encounters with seasons – and the cultural customs cannot be learned with just one trip – several trips are required even to get a glimpse. But imagine you had no idea HOW you got there – imagine just waking up with your stream of consciousness in that new land, with no frame of reference of the previous land that had raised you up. What would that be like?

I think we know – since the moment we are born, in whatever land we are born in, we have no previous framework of what was present before us – we have no HOW to HOW we woke up in the first place – and not having a given how, is what drives our quest for meaning. It's truly the driving force behind the collective build-up, of the countless HOW'S, that have scattered their way into our present day meaning of *how the world works*. Which we have always accepted.

Once HOW arose, the human species began searching for the answer – it's actually what created the human species in the first place. Even the idea of being able to produce a word, that could then be released from the mouth, with tonalities of flux and influx a new positioning of the lips – which then stretch themselves out in a wave of sound – into the ears of another, while at the same time *spark* a meaning or a question that BOTH understand – is truly mind blowing.

Posing a question is one thing, and over time, became very easy for our species to manage. Unfortunately, we are very limited with our means of actually searching for the HOW answer to many of the why questions we are likely to propose.

Everything changed with *fire*.

Something about bringing light to night releases the fight or flight allowing new sight in the depths of fright breaking through with might causing new delight that only light from night allows for *new height*.

Fire gave humans an inside look into the heart of the sun – into the depths of creation where the soul of life burned with blazing fire. It was captivating to look at, warming the skin when surroundings were cold – but more importantly, it was fire that changed the very structure of whatever it touched, creating new forms to exist – *fire is the catalyst to all evolution on earth.*

But through the comet of life or the asteroid of death – each cycle of fire brings about a new change or era in the grand order of what is considered to be right or wrong yes or no dead or alive.

Any person who claims to be right, must in some form, whether they admit it or not, also think another claim is wrong in the counter-claim form to their own point of view, from that which they feel is inherently a correct claim on whatever they are claiming to be right.

Obviously this very sentence, the sentence that was just written, then transcends itself back to the very creation of its birth, only posing the questionable sentence to its own self as a sentence: is the sentence that created the sentence in the first place a correct sentence? If not, how did I even become able to ask myself, as the sentence that I am, the sentence that was just written, if I'm even a real sentence

– if I was not a real sentence, would I have even been able to ask myself if I was a sentence in the first place? To think therefore *I am.*

It's almost like a human finding out they are human, but only to later ask them self if they are in fact human. You're not asking yourself if you are a fish or a reptile, because hundreds of millions ago, when we actually were fish and reptiles, we were unable to pose these questions to the self – it is our unique ability as Human Beings to understand *the very first level of consciousness*: asking yourself what in fact you are – hence being truly alive.

This is the essence of the binary method of coding that all life originates from. A simple yes or no answer – a one or a zero – *alive or not alive*: that really is the answer to the self-posed question, that all live begins from.

Yet understanding one question only leads us to then ask the next question of human evolution – what was before the beginning of what we have just claimed as the beginning. The loop of questioning extends itself into the finite level of the quark and the grandeur scale of the multiverse – or – from the very sentence that was posed earlier, to the paragraph that embodies it, the page that holds it, the chapter that it resides in, to the very book that created it.

Obviously one could continue with the line of reasoning back to the beginning or of course the end…

Nevertheless, it is only natural to know that there will never be an end to our questioning – therefore there will never be an end to the answers in which we come up with to answer the new questions posed, which then begins to transcend our meaning of time itself. No end to questioning leads to no end in answers – which leads to no end in time. I guess the goal of our species, and it really is the pathway to evolving the mind: *Ask a question that no one has ever asked before* – it is only our nature to find the answer – hence building new platforms that allow for our children to stand upon: *creating a new generation.*

# Berlin

This was a mere slice, from a larger piece of writings that Amstel was focused on. He was now living in Berlin for over a year, studying the language, and working as a bartender in one of the many, underground-electronic-warehouse clubs the city is known for. Of course he wasn't alone in the city – he had made countless connections along the way – crossing all boundaries of race, ethnicity, gender and sexual orientation. On any given week, he would find himself meeting up with one friend here, another *brother* there – finding new friends and brothers along the way.

His path to Berlin, which after *three months of allowing* himself to fully experience what Berlin actually is, had become his new home. It was filled with so much intrigue and new experiences for him – along with the most interesting people he had ever met. It wasn't until he arrived in Berlin that he was TRULY able to have the conversations he so desired in life. Conversations rich in connection and sharing, where the very soul of humanity spoke through the words, showing itself in the warmest of fashions. Surprisingly enough, although he was focused on learning German, Amstel was privileged enough to find himself with the greatest English speakers he had ever spoken with – he had to go to Berlin to fully understand his own language. Through twisted tonalities of accented words, Amstel found himself having to REALLY listen to what people said, and in those moments, he found himself, for the first time – fully engaged in the moment at hand – allowing a *higher level of understanding* to unfold.

It was a never ending learning process for Amstel – not being accustomed to such truthful and deep meaning conversations, only pushed him to engage at levels, which at first scared him, but like anything else in this world – if you're afraid in the beginning – you're most likely on the right path. Amstel might have been nervous at times, sometimes even completely lost – yet in his heart, in his mind and soul he knew, that lost and found are of the same.

He accepted the principle that others have something to offer – others have something to teach, but only to those willing to learn – only to those willing to *accept an offering.* On any given week, of any given day, Amstel was more than willing to accept an offering. Yet the very idea of acceptance, especially to something unrestricted like an offering, is always a two-way-street – the true offering only arises when BOTH offer, and through that – a mutual acceptance arises. No matter the situation, Amstel found himself ready to offer; whether it was accepted or not, was never under his control. The only thing in control was whether or not he accepted another's offering; which he usually did. Therefore, he found himself on the foreground of some of the deepest truths imaginable – beginning his experiences of understanding what he found to be most important in this world – other peoples perspectives.

* * *

A colorful kitchen surrounds Amstel on a mid-summer's night in Berlin. He glances around the kitchen: *a single wall* is splashed with fiery undertones of red and orange mixed with streaks of pink and yellow, which focus themselves in a circular pattern toward the center of the wall – the sun was setting – the night was about to begin. The corner of the wall which is mostly yellow at this point, has an image of a tree, painted as a shadowy silhouette – it's leaves already fallen from the freezing Berlin winter, and its branches stretch out like arms toward the light, crisscrossing themselves in every direction. A string of hanging bulbs arch their way across the wall, giving the tree a subtle glow, which when combined with the red-orange coloration, simply allowed the kitchen to resonate in warm sunlight. Although Amstel was currently living in this apartment – with its sunrise-sunset-kitchen-wall, it wasn't until tonight that he finally saw just how spectacular his kitchen was – he was truly blown away.

"Verstehst du?" a voice projects itself to Amstel, breaking his concentration on the wall.

"What, I mean *was*?" Amstel looks to the four others sitting in the kitchen alongside him, "Sorry, I wasn't really listening, what's going on?" He chuckles a bit.

They all laugh, peering deeply to one another – Alice, the one who asked Amstel if he understood what was being said, continues, "You have to learn German Amstel." She glances quickly to him.

"Believe me I know" he replies, "I mean, I am in B1 of my German course – but you just speak so quickly that… well, it's hard to keep up at times."

"Auf Deutsch bitte…?" she says, continuing her smile and wanting him to say what he just said in German, with a please of course.

"See that's the thing," Amstel thinks for a bit, "for me to say what I just said in German………… well" he takes a long pause, trying to gather his words, "That's going to take a long time I think. It's like as much as I'm learning right now, and it's a lot, but for me to speak fluidly and not have to think about what I'm saying, *which is really the only way to speak* – I just think it will take years to get to that level."

Alice allows what he said to soak in, then she replies, "But if you don't start practicing, you never get to that point."

Amstel nods, "Yea very true," he continues, "I guess it's like the ultimate catch 22 for me…"

Alice shakes her head looking lost with that analogy – Amstel explains, "I want to be part of the conversation obviously – but the only way that I really want to be part of any conversation is if I don't have to think about what I'm saying – or having to translate what I want to say from English to German – or vice versa in terms of my understanding. So it's like where do I begin, if I start speaking in German, I'm only going to say very basic basic things, but what if *what's in my mind is not basic*, then I'm not really getting to express what I want to express – catch 22."

"Slow down!" Alice laughs, as do the others.

"Yea it's all good" Amstel refocuses and then continues… "Ich kann nur ein bisschen Deutsch sprechen – aber meistens, kann ich es besser *verstehen* als sprechen, und wenn ich etwas nicht auf Deutsch sagen kann – Dann, sage ich auf English."

Alice's eyebrows raise rapidly, her eyes grow big "Whoa! Seeeeee… very good!" Alice quickly responds, "I understand perfectly… you can only speak a little bit of German, but mostly you *understand* than speaking, and when you cannot say something in German, you say in English – Wow! Very good, I'm impressed." The others in the group seemed to be a little shocked as well, Alice continues, "Please start speaking more German with us." She smiles to him.

Amstel laughs a bit, "Thanks! But that means you have to start speaking more English with me!"

Alice's warmth begins to fade, "No." She suddenly says, breaking the connection to Amstel and focuses her attention to a burning candle at the center of the table, her face like stone.

*Alice* was one of the key people who aided Amstel in connecting with everyone around him, especially when Amstel seemed lost and confused. Although for Amstel, he never really felt all that confused – he just simply never focused that hard on what people were saying – mostly he created in his own mind his own conversations which seemed to always fit with what he wanted to be said in any particular moment – but this was not the truth. It seemed for Alice, she was adamant on bringing Amstel into the truth of the conversations that seemed to be the cornerstone of the culture.

Alice herself was quite the enigma to most, however, Amstel figured out fairly quickly who she was: a lost soul who felt she would never be found. Her ups and downs seemed to be a natural therapy for her, sharing each *up* moment through her smiles and laughs, yet showing her *downs* through the frowns, tears and aggression toward those outside her circle. Alice was a fire-cracker with a short fuse – and those with too much light, seemed to always set her off. A new hairstyle one week, flowed into a new tattoo the following, which all seemed to create new truths of her own self-image. She was constantly re-inventing herself, trying desperately to improve the negative perception she had on herself and reality; yet still remaining true to who she was. Her acceptance of the idea that she would never be found was a blessing and a curse – only because it allowed for her to always stay truthful, no matter what her mood might be – while at the same time, damning her to create her own personal hell. Alice was truly a self-torturing soul, finding moments in life that only seemed to further her own acceptance that she was cursed, while never appreciating the moments showing her to be blessed. However, this darker side to Alice never seemed to phase Amstel – who mostly saw within the darker confounds, the individual light still peeking through – a game of peek-a-boo was never out of the question for Alice – but it seemed her constant battle within, on whether to have her hands up or down, was always on her mind – hence creating her *wall from within.*

Alice was obsessed with her own story; lost in wonderland – yet unable to realize the magic of wonderland. Her fall down the rabbit's whole began when she was a child: a distant mother combined with an overpowering sister created a *lost father* in her heart. The turmoil within, only fed the fire that forced her to begin her self-medicating ways at a very early age. Never allowing her true self to form the truth of who her true self actually was. By the age of seventeen, she had seen more than most seventy year olds with her ability to perceive the world around her. Sex drugs and electronic music became her escape – yet she was powerless in determining what she was actually escaping from. Feelings of doubt, created confusion within her thoughts – which seemed to only become heightened to new extremes when she decided to heighten herself to new extremes; of which she made a constant habit of doing.

Alice found connection only to those in a higher realm of thought – which for her, was a base level, yet allowed her a transcendence into the mind of others. She understood what people think, by the manner in which they behave, showing its truth in the subtle actions and reactions by those who she allowed herself to connect with. This was a powerful power that she was powerless to control. However, she slowly brought herself to break away from the false fathers who preached false messages of unfulfilling truth. But this took time for her – and with time comes a price to pay – which takes its toll in the age in which she finally developed her proper surroundings through the people who finally began to care for her, allowing her gifts to flourish.

Alice breaks her concentration to the flame resting at the center of the table. The others, including Amstel, respect her moment of reflection through silence. She looks to Amstel, almost apologetic with the rolling of her eyes and shaking of her head, allowing him to see that she lost herself through her own reflection – in which Amstel was no stranger in doing himself. By four o'clock in the morning the group has dissipated from four to two, leaving Amstel and Alice alone in the sun-blazed kitchen – they look to each other in a semi-quick glance, Amstel unaware of what to say only nods his head, sparking Alice to create the only question she could...... "How's Sofia?"

Amstel smiles.

* * *

After three days along the coast, Amstel finally reaches Yosemite, forgetting his *desires of having the perfect tent*. His time with the surf couple was enlightening – once again reminding him the reasons of leaving his Venice Beach home in the first place: all smiles and no cries simply lacked the essence of what Amstel believed to be the truth of life. He left the surfers completely aware of who they were through their *unawareness* of who he was.

Although who we are is a continually changing idea with the image of ourselves that we project to others – there are those, who for whatever reasons, do not allow the surface to change – hence ceasing the change from within. Not that outside reflects from within – but in some sense it does. It's imperfection that creates true perfection, yet if what we receive from others is a picture perfect idea of the picture perfect life – then what? Everything is perfect, and we might as well just die, since there is no movement to our journey. We need outside forces to push and pull us, displacing our form in time and space, allowing us to create new paths to walk on – paths that are difficult, challenging, adventurous and above all unclear to the exact outcome that will take place. Perfect is easy – perfect is clear – perfect is dangerous: you could live an entire life with perfection – only to realize you never really did anything in life – only to wake up at the brink of death and wallow in regret of a life that was deemed "the perfect life." Perfection might be in the eye of the beholder – but principles follow from this – the Parthenon, the image of Greek perfection is built with imperfect columns – yet it's through this imperfect structure that allows perfection to stand. The older we get in life, the more this becomes clear – through our own faded image of our personal reflection we gain clarity on that which matters most: our personal story.

Or in the case of Amstel – *her personal story.*

# Sofia

"Will you marry me?"

She asks with the sincerest undertone of melodic deep affection that Amstel's eyebrows can't help but to raise – her face, gently glowing from the string of winter lights hanging amongst the trees, is strikingly featured with the highest cheekbones he had ever seen; flushed harmoniously into pouty lips that when cracked, reveal an imperfect smile with the faintest gap between her teeth. She looks so deeply to him, almost sad with her gaze, which penetrates him to his core. Her sandy-blonde hair gently falls on her face, creating a true picture of beauty unfolding before his eyes.

He tries to speak, yet at this very moment he is speechless, unable to determine his own feelings of love. What is love he thinks, as he looks to the face that is reaching out – longing for his affection. Within a millisecond, every previous relationship comes flooding into his mind – each only showing their sparkling times – each, only a phantom yet relived as truth, haunting his mind with ideas of doubt.

Sofia's eyes, deep blue in nature with patterns of grey, quietly fill with tears, revealing to him her love. Amstel looks to her, wanting to say the overwhelming YES he so desires, where reaching for the sky with feelings of over-joyous-joy becomes his new – yet he cannot. He has too many thoughts in his mind and simply cannot put them into category of priority. He continues his deepest look of love to her, truthful in feeling, yet confused in thought – he finally is able to mutter:

"Let's keep walking…"

She looks to him, accepting the man that he is and knowing *he simply doesn't understand who she is yet.* He's still lost within his own perspective – unable to remove himself from his self – he's replaced lost with his own interpretation of found, which somehow involves only his own interpretation on interpreting the interpretations that only he thinks he can interpret.

Each tree reminds Amstel of the kitchen; missing the leaves to spread the wings of captured light. Bundles of dead foliage perfectly piled up capture his attention, where the very idea that his path may follow the same trajectory – only to become one of many, piled upon the ground, losing the ability to retain his light – begins to frighten him. This bundle of dead leaves is his sign – only to become like the others – dead and rotting in a pile of those just like him – how could he possibly go through with this?

* * *

Sofia's ability to simplify her thoughts to the absolute minimum, where the core understanding of truth was just that: *true,* was the gift she gave to the world. Sofia thought and spoke in riddles – without ever knowing she was riddling her own riddle. To those who understood, answers to questions people never even knew they had asked, would be answered – in the simplest form imaginable: words.

At a very young age, Sofia had become obsessed with words; in all forms they found themselves arranging in. She read countless books and played many types of word games, everything she could possibly get her hands onto, which sparked her interest at levels that *very few could understand*. Her parents were more than happy, for by the age of twelve, Sofia had already read close to five hundred books – including all of the classic fictions, genres of philosophy, time-era pieces and her absolute favorite: *Autobiographical*. She became cross-cultured with her reading, branching off from German literature into English and American style writings – enveloping herself on a daily basis; reading and writing her thoughts down onto complete-page-filled diaries. It was never enough for Sofia, until one day – she just stopped reading.

She went to the bookstore, having just finished a book of a thousand pages and simply couldn't find the next one to begin. She searched for hours – almost finishing entire books but then finally realizing the book just wasn't for her. She would read introductions and first chapters, reading the forewords and sometimes even the conclusions – yet no matter how much she tried to begin her next book, something was off, something was no longer connecting with the love she once had for reading. She went home from the bookstore feeling feelings that twisted her insides to new levels that she was not adept to feeling. It was almost as if her skin began to crawl – an itch began to surface deep within her soul, and slowly began to slither its way throughout her body – breaching itself, barricading its essence in her right forearm. All of her insecurities and doubts of who she is and was became focused on her arm. At dinner with her family:

> Mother and father talk while sisters listen yet here I am unable to talk unable to listen.

What could she possibly do? Everything became dark for her – feelings once experienced were no longer experienced – the sun shining no longer shined – music that had once filled her soul now told her she had no soul - she became nothing within her own mind, nothing within the mind of others, nothing nothing nothing was her only something.

> She no longer found herself crying.
> She no longer found herself sighing.
> She no longer found herself surviving.

As she wraps the towel around her wet body, looking in the mirror at a self no longer connected to itself, she begins to scratch her arm. Without realizing, her arm begins to bleed, a deep scratch seething at the surface – her fingernails tainted with the blood from her own body – she focuses intently on her arm, which looks so different than it had before; it looks alive. Through the pain she now has connection – through the pain she begins to cry…

… Through the pain she sees how to survive.

Never letting the scab heal was the source of beginning pleasures – yet no matter how many times she picked her arm, every round of pain only found a new level of healing – until finally there was no longer a scab to pick, just the faintest of scars, showcasing the dim moments of control once controlled – yet uncontrollable to actually control.

Talks amongst her family on politics, economic problems, hatred of Nazis and her mother's work as a doctor did absolutely nothing for Sofia, as her arm continually itched with indifferent feelings of sorrow. She found herself constantly in a state of anxiety – nervous to be around others – ashamed to show her arm, which at this point was completely healed, no scar to detect. She found herself at these family dinners, listening to a pattern of words that only revealed the rhythm of speech to her – no content to latch onto and decipher a *deeper meaning of truth which is undiscovered by most* – where was the puzzle of understanding she constantly thought? Her family was a master of presenting completed puzzles, with no attachment to the process of said puzzle. The questions of thought were only provoked by the school curriculum and the level of schooling each of the girls was at – Sofia being the oldest was constantly having to back track, stooping back down to the lower levels that her family presented as higher. What was the point on talking about your day, unless you actually want to talk about your day?

Creating talks just to talk diminishes the actual ability to talk on ideas you want to talk about if you feel your deeper talks will just be categorized into the typical talk that most are accustomed to understand. Yet Sofia knew there was a deepness to her family – Sofia knew her sisters understood like her, as did her mother and father. It was the notion of blocking this deepness of growth that got under Sofia's skin – literally.

Battles began to rage between Sofia and *her father*; who mostly thought she was trying too hard to be an outcast. He constantly would force Sofia to be involved in these conversations *she really felt no attachment to* – only creating a burning fire of hatred within the soul of a young woman who began to lose her desire to fight back. Whenever she would begin to respond with a level of truth – it seemed she was attacked from all directions – Her mother, only backing up her father, in which both thought THIS was the correct way: constantly active, learning through the school curriculum, fighting set establishment and never showing ones true sadness.

It was this particular denial of truth that really got to Sofia – for although the other cores of learning and fighting systems are correct, if the truth of who you are at any particular moment just happens to be sad – then you can still be who you are – still learning and fighting for you rights, while also being in that moment of sadness. However, for her parents and the idea of showing the sun-always-shinning puzzle, this is where most of the conflict arose: everyone is happy – everyone is smiling. This of course is not truth.

Sofia was unable scratch her un-scratchable scratch, causing her weekly visits to the bathroom, where she found herself face to face with her own reflection. At first her cuts only scratched the surface – fragile lines of softly mutilated skin seemed to suffice – but the pains of sorrow began to grow deeper, only furthering her cuts to grow.

Fragile lines became distinct trenches, where only the next pattern of hollows would satiate Sofia's desire of connection, fueling desires of completion. At night she would lie in bed, feeling her wounds and dreaming of the next cuts to come. Slowly her self-drawn map of self-inflicting pain began to engulf her, no longer finding an appropriate place to draw out her new wave of sorrow. For whatever reasons, she was self-contained enough to keep her cuts to the part of her body actually calling out to be cut: her forearm. When space was no longer available – she began to recut her cuts; inflicting a higher level of pain to unfold. Heightened by this new level only dragged her sorrow beyond the limits of depression, causing complete dependency on her only perceptible source of feeling: her cutting. The cycle consumed her.

It was this cycle that Amstel was able to see transcribed against her skin, as the tattoo she got later only removed the focus, yet the scars still remained to those who understood what to look for – Amstel knew exactly what these scars represented and was even more captivated by the beautiful girl who bore them on her forearm.

* * *

Amstel continues his stare at the bundle of dead, dried leaves, only thinking to himself:

How can I go through with this?

Suddenly, Sofia's dog *Emmie*, a German-Shepherd-Saint-Bernard mix pounces her way into the pile of leaves – digging her face deep and destroying the perfection that WAS the pile. She picks her head up, her body completely submerged beneath the bundle, where a single leaf lies perfectly placed upon her forehead. She peers deeply into Amstel – her expression, playful in manner yet serious in nature, resonates profoundly with him as he remembers his first day in berlin:

> The day Amstel Arrived, he had already been backpacking his way through Europe for several months, traveling as cheaply as possible and staying in youth hostels along the way. He had not seen Sofia since the airport – yet the communication was always there – writing each other almost every day, and sharing the experiences each had, without the other experiencing the exact same experience the other was experiencing. Arriving in Berlin was not as simple as simply arriving in Berlin. For Amstel, it was arriving at a new destination – a new point in his life – where commitment to this beautiful girl would be his mission. Through thick and thin, better or for worse – *til death were to do them part*, was already in his mind as he waited to be picked up. Suffice it to say, Amstel was quite nervous to see Sofia again, but could only power through his anxious thoughts of apprehension.
>
> As he lugs his giant suitcase into the narrow hallway, a ferocious bark bounces between the walls – shaking the very structure of the apartment's foundation.

Where Emmie's inability to even look at Amstel causes overwhelming feelings of misplacement and doubt, sending Amstel into a confusing despair. As he looks to Emmie, who suddenly looks away, staring up to Sofia with her giant eyes and golden brown hair – her head resting gently on Sofia's lap – it becomes too much for Amstel – he suddenly breaks down, unable to catch his breath, having a panic attack in the middle of the fire-blazed kitchen. Sofia rushes to his side, comforting him and understanding that everything is just too much – Emmie also focuses on Amstel and begins her ability to realize exactly who he is, which takes several weeks of daily walks and extra treats just to allow for Amstel to scratch her stomach – yet overtime, the two would become inseparable – changing Amstel's fundamental ideas of what it is to even be a dog – where the path of unity we as humans walk, eventually returns back to the oneness that dogs and other animals alike share – living daily in the essence of love is the nature of Emmie, as only love can be understood as the universal language of connecting across all barriers and species – allowing for a flourishing relationship and total understanding to unfold.

*"Let's just make this work..."* He says to Sofia, whose eyes are still filled with tears, as they continue their walk around the Platz – Emmie still immersed within the pile of leaves. He looks deeply to her, trying to share as much as possible, yet unable to say more than that which was just spoken.

Sofia's thoughts suddenly begin to fragment as she remembers the fight they had earlier that day:

Reliving the idea of almost breaking apart, witnessing a side to him never seen before – cold and dark – distant and callous – blank within the eyes. This side was no longer sided for it had become his whole, consuming him to the depths of hell, where the devil himself would bow down – giving him the power he so desired. This man, now proclaiming his will to make this work, was not this man earlier.

Yet we did NOT break apart. The desires to grow within each other still burn brightly – as though the dual sided nature of man can be overthrown – giving way to new understandings of what it is to even be a man.

of what it is to be loved.
of what it is to accept love.
of what it is to return the love to that which is loved.

Once the path is followed, you need to be true to where the path actually leads. Giving yourself completely and selflessly to the ideas that unfold. *The single life* path has already ran its course – it brought him to me – where it was I that found him – lost in a world of confusion and utter denial of the truth that this world actually holds.

I shared with him the truth – giving him all of my deepest secrets, sharing my body mind and soul, crying countless tears along the way. Held him in his darkest moments – cradled his very being with the warmth that only I could provide. Listened to every word he spoke and understood him at levels he himself couldn't understand, while only making clear the understanding that would become under- stood. I sat in silence with him, peering at a face that looked scared and dark, only to give him all my light. Brightening his core beyond that of a star – allow- ing him to see within the darkest of dark – sharing with him the energy of the universe through the sim- ple breath of my lips – continually filling his core, allowing him to burst through his own skin, only to emerge as the beautiful butterfly that I knew that he was, know that he is… Why doesn't he want to fly?

*How cannot he not see this?*

It's almost as if he forgets the entire two years we've been together and the moments that were shared at the levels that only he and I could share.

Only he and I could see.
Only he and I have witnessed.

If there were to be someone else… there would have been someone else. His ideas of the potential some- one else are complete imaginary sequences of thought that only serve to confuse. But it's almost as if he seeks the confusion – searching for ideas that remove him from the beautiful life he has found – bringing him back into the darkness where only chaos and disorder arise. Is this a guy thing, or an Amstel thing? I know I've never met anybody like him; never had such a beautiful man show me his inner most workings, explaining to me without explaining to me who he really is; never seeing such a purity to spirit, such a carefree manner in which to behave – but I've also seen the exact opposite in this man. A man completely taken back to the basic – hormonal crazed in desire – an animal in thought – a man seeking pleasure through his senses, where the visual sense is king. And I understand this side to him – I've worn his lingerie leggings and positioned my body the way he likes – posing for him and only for him, but is there an end to these sexual exploits? Is this not just the very basic caveman ideology – grunting and moaning to please the self in the easiest way possible?

How is that growth?

But I love him – more than anything I love him. I want to spend the rest of my life with him, building together a life that we share – *but is that possible for him?* Can he remove himself from himself and be there for ME and for the family I know we could eventually grow together?

I think we share the same thoughts at times… complete understanding of a particular moment at its deepest and highest level. Yet as I look to share that experience of understanding and further its meaning, I sometimes find myself having to babysit – as if this is the very first time he's ever understood such a thought or experience. He can be so innocent at times – so childish in nature – and perceptible to outside forces. Yet something about him just continually draws me to him – wanting to re-experience everything I know we have. It's almost as if we have to re-build our entire relationship at times – because he just forgets. Or doesn't hold on as strongly as he needs to. But he's trying. I know he's trying. And most importantly… I know he loves me!

I'll never give up on him and somehow, I know he knows this and understands what this love represents; knowing I free him beyond his wildest ideas of freedom – not freedom in the sense of a single man who claims to be free – but the actual freedom of the mind. I just think for him though, he doesn't want to be free in his mind, he would rather loop his thoughts back into his thoughts, creating the twists and turns I so often see his mind taking – why does he do this? *I know there's a creativity to him*, something immeasurable except for the measures he himself creates on what it is that he himself can measure – but what do the inner-twisted thoughts on a fragmented reality have to do with being creative?

At times I feel like he's forgotten his own path of redemption; forgetting the very moments in life that brought him to where he is; forgetting the pain associated with these moments and somehow thinking they weren't what they were. Very few in life get the calling to leave home and explore what the world has to offer – and even fewer find a love that really is the cornerstone of acceptance. Acceptance of the past, but more importantly – acceptance of not changing where it is that you have accepted to accept as your final acceptance. To find acceptance at all levels of questions the self so often asks is the gift that I give to him – I just don't think he's always accepting what I KNOW deep down he already has accepted!

The two of them continue their walk around the beautifully glowing walkway – locked in the other's embrace, completely glued to the movement of the other, walking in rhythm and captivated by the street's glow, Sofia continues.

"I just know I love you more than anything and I really do want to spend the rest of my life with you."

Amstel is taken back… of course those words had been spoken before – every love story has a version of these words – yet the difference for him came with the one saying it, as he's finally able to connect the words with an actual person. He looks to her, there's such a serene beauty to her face, a calming love that soothes his very essence; reaching deep within him and pulling him toward the light. His thoughts suddenly go away and he finds himself face to face with that which is most beautiful. He looks deep to her, caressing her face and kissing her forehead, holding each other under the glowing trees as if the entire universe is lighting them up.

"I love you more than anything too, Sofia … let's get married!!"

# The fourth Dimension

To be able to decide or not to be able to decide – *that really is the question.*

Yet if we understand the idea that the very idea of new decisions to be made really stem from an already understood idea of what the answer is in terms of the idea of all possible decisions to be made, then we clearly see *the decision is whatever you decide the decision to actually be*, yet only understood through the decision's ability to transform itself into the different answers each possible decision creates.

*It's the fifth dimensional outlet* of understanding each circumstance with its own set of complete answers – each un-connected to each, since each is separate from each. Yet through the un-connected set of different thought-streams of fourth-dimensional-time-loop-possibilities, each understood in its entirety and decided separately as though the very decision within this thought stream is the only answer possible within said decision, we again see clearly the truth waiting at its core: *The decisions needed to be decided are already decided* – they're simply not experienced until your third-dimensional-living-in-the-moment-self reaches its fourth-dimensional-time-loop-self: which understands each decision needed to be made by breaking into the fifth dimension where all possibilities on all decisions to be made becomes witnessed by the fourth in the fifth to be shared with the third.

Like the spiral breaking the barrier of the second dimension into the third to become its spherical three dimensional form – we too must break our own third to tap into the fourth which has already understood everything revolving around the fifth – trusting the fourth, for it understands far beyond what you yourself can ever comprehend being trapped in the third.

Yet through this trust in the fourth… the walls of the third come crashing down… freeing yourself to experience yourself in all possible dimensions.

Creating the catalyst-loop the fourth creates: bringing the third into the fifth: Experiencing 2UP from the 1UP form of 1UP. Where the third dimension's self's abilities of understanding begin to expand far beyond what was deemed possible for expansion within the third. Continually combining the levels of accomplished UP understandings, *losing your very own counting of the numbers*, creating deep within the self the purity of your UP-self-itself, and accepting all levels as the continual progress of what it is to even go UP.

> A 1/5th possibility: The easiest path taken is always the path that *leads one back* to the original path which created the separate paths of understanding the different paths that can unfold in the first place. Going deep on one's own deepness of one's own ability to be led back creates only one direct possibility of a

path that is *not actually chosen* yet can be understood without the choosing of said path: going back is only an option to be thought on – it's never an option to choose.

2/5<sup>th</sup> possibilities: Understanding the idea that to say "never" to an option to choose, only limits one to one actual option: the option opposite to that of the never chosen path. But to have a never chosen path, only because at the first level of understanding the path, one cannot break into its second option of understanding there is no such thing as never, leads one to the second possibility: It's only an option to choose never if the decision was made to choose never, but only understood as the choice that it is – and choices always have two possibilities.

3/5<sup>th</sup> possibilities: Having the wisdom to understand that "always" limits the two choices that are thought of as never choosing, or possibly choosing, to just that: the two options of never or the opposite of never. But understanding that it still falls in the same realm of the same possibilities taking course, leads to a third: each option of choice is the same – whether never going back is the decision where never truly is the one possibility chosen, or the second of going back is decided – the idea of understanding the two within their own realms of meaning is what the third possibility is understood as: a choice of two, leads to your actual decision which is only third in the hierarchy of total possibilities.

4/5$^{th}$ possibilities: *The truth lies here* – for after understanding the first level of: simply deciding never, to moving on towards the idea of: choosing the opposite of that initially never chosen path, to then understanding each option on its own with its very own choice to choose – we then reach the fourth once again: the actual truth of what is chosen, since all levels: from never to opposite of never – and everything in between – is finally understood at the level it needs to be understood: allowing for the path to simply choose the path that is now already chosen as the path that is the chosen path… Sofia.

Amstel was unable to continue his writing on what a five-fifths possibility was, since there would be no way to ever break free from his fourth dimension-time looped self.

Or so he thought…

# Tripping

Before there was a proposal and before there was doubt, Sofia and Amstel had taken *several trips together…*

FROM a ten day snowboarding trip in the deep mountains of Czech Republic; where Sofia's sister and her friends were open enough to allow Amstel to sit in a single chair for seven hours – lost in his mind, thinking of god the universe and understanding truths unimaginable before – he even came up with his next essay idea entitled *I am God*.

The others played board games; laughing and deepening their bonds with one another. Sofia read a book of a thousand pages…

TO simple weekend getaways in the countryside of Germany – surrounded by giant willowing trees and blossoming flowers in unchartered fields of golden wheat.

It seemed each trip conjoined itself to overlap from the previous experience. So by the time Sofia and Amstel had finally reached the point of traveling through Europe in a VW, the amount of overlapping *trip-experiences* was strong – including three Music Festivals, monthly concerts, weekly open airs and of course the nightly bar scene; which technically were electronic clubs. The music always captivating… the music always alive.

Two weeks after *Fusion*, one of Germany's biggest Festivals, Sofia and Amstel would leave for their VW trip through Europe; which was actually Sofia's second trip – the first being when she was nineteen and was gone for six months with a guy, who by the end of *their trip,* had formed his newly formed dreads. Amstel had no idea what to expect – but would definitely return, hair filled with dreads, the beard of a lumber-*JACK*, and more importantly – the thoughts that would eventually break them apart.

* * *

<u>*The boat ride in Amsterdam*</u>:

> Several cafes experienced where people watching
>> comes alive,
> each with their own experience, their life showcased
>> through the eyes.
> Moments of connection trigger deep within your
>> mind,
> as you create your own story keeping the details
>> inside.
>
> The sun is about to set and glowing ripples fill the
>> water,
> while street lights turn on showing a father and his
>> daughter.
> He holds her close with a smile upon his face,
> it's so easy to see the beauty in this place.

As we enter the boat friendly faces filled with warmth,
it's Sofia's love that rocks me back and forth.
The boat begins to move and no more words are
 spoken,
as we set sail through the city... *nothing is ever broken.*

Light particles dance as they reflect their inner
 workings,
centered on the water, our bodies no longer jerking.
In-stoned in the moment everything becomes clear:
*life is a gift ... let yourself to be here.*

One cannot **twist thoughts** when light combines
 with water,
as you suddenly see the same father and his daughter.
This time with mother, being the family they are,
NOW thoughts become twisted as you remember
 past scars.

Am I to have a family... am I really the type?
To give myself selflessly and remove my-selfish-type.
To be there for her and only for her,
then to have family and only for them.

## NO MORE SENSE – NO MORE RHYME AND REASON

How is this okay if I'm constantly UN - okay?
I know right now she's looking a t me.
Wanting to m ake sure everything is serene.
But for whatever re asons I simp ly cannot be... the
 man that I know she want me to be.

Why o' why? Do I have such stupid issues.

With love and be ing loved I'm constantly needing
tissues. *Not 4 me*......... since its rare that I cry.
But for the hearts that I b r e a k... and the tears from
the i r I's ---
Am I horrible for the twisted thoughts that come in
side?
the thoughts of *lust and desire* and wanting to be
"that guy"

How easy it is for those who don't care – they live life care
free and do what they dare.

But there's NO TRUTH in this... NO TRUTH
from this lie...
How do I know...... you were... "THIS GUY!"

You live d it for long... and lived it fore real... constantly looking for the next best deal. Looking for aces in every hand of
poker......... is simply the way to <u>NEVER PLAY poke-her.</u>

Look at her and see her here – already with the subtle tear
– thoughts bombarding thru ur ears – never looking in a
mirror – feeling doubt combined with fear – god I wish I
had a beer – call me john I'm feeling dear – how easy it is
to just be queer.

If you think she doesn't know than it's you who's mistaken.
WAIT she's still here, maybe she's ... miss-taken

Mistaken 4 seeing what she thou ght she saw......

Its easy to see I'm a man
of straw.
no back bone inside laughing
ha-ha-ha
sucking on mothers t-ee-t screaming 4 my lost
BA-BA
but really … where the hell is my ma-ma.
*prolly at home smoking some of that gan-JAH*
l OO k at me…… my smile now a
FROWN! LOOK AT ME!
…… I'm a fucking clown --- my only color brown.

My head spinning round and round…spiraling hysterically down down-down.

Afraid to leave the ground -------------- unable to hear sound ------ lost and never found--
---- constantly feeling bound ----

How can this boat ride       NOW       be so long gone?

A constant taste of DIS-grace sp L itting outta my face no way to win this race I'm in last place simply a basket-case with no basket or case an angel without his grace my shoes have no lace unable to embrace everything that's taken place thinking back at first base or home without a trace should this be UPPER or lower case worst-case in case I get encased in hitler's white race I'll simply escape to my imaginary place which happens to be in deep interstellar space which really is the *higher place*………

# What is wrong with me???

Oh wait……

Could it be the weed?

I think this is what they call tripping……       Literally.

*The deserted beach in Belgium's North Sea*:

It was easy for me to see that life could be serenely serene – no more thoughts from me seeming to distance me from me being me – only way to be is to just be free from the tyranny of constantly finding the key – please stop pleading for the insanity plea or trying to guarantee your own sanity – 1 2 3 isn't as easy as A B C but music's do-re-mi can somehow free – Sofia right now is the dancing-queen – ankle deep in the sun-setting-sea being completely free and showing me life can really be this easy – as we begin to see our beautiful little Emmie running so beautifully – unable to determine her own velocity she simply runs full speed into me – as I chase her with glee the birds scatter and flee leaving Emmie and me feeling just a bit lonely – as we look back to our queen who's still dancing so free embracing this life and this beautifully-serene-scene – I can't help but to capture exactly what I see as I reach for my camera which has been hiding from me – the sun constantly setting in front of me means the pictures themselves are just a little shadowy – yet light beams where it needs as her smile still exceeds what I ever thought it could be – she's so beautiful to me which is apparently seen as the easy way to see that life can be lived so harmoniously – no reason to think deeply on what thinking deeply means since we really only know our own meaning to things – this is what she teaches me as the teacher she be never really knowing her own teachings to me – as we finally see the sun blissfully leave we begin to kiss ever-so-delicately – as I caress her soft cheek and begin to peer deep it's her love that begins to elevate me – while standing on Belgium's empty North Sea *Sofia is becoming the one for me.*

I wish this could be my everlasting eternity – flying so free towards the infinite stretch of infinity – hand and hand we see there's nobody but we – yet I'm constantly searching for who else wants my ring – is this the way to be free from the torment and misery constantly coming over me – everything can be seen as a moment to see yet momentarily I only see how I'm actually seen – wondering what people are thinking of me even though it's only we on this beach in Belgium's North Sea – and those who know me know I'm crazy including Sofia and Emmie who still somehow accept me *allowing me to be free.*

But can WE overpower the ME that is apparently seen as only ME that's even existing to be – *its only through accepting* the theory of WE transcending my ME to WE allowing ME to be free with WE that WE can be free from the tyranny of ME – constantly thinking of ME is no way to be but there's no guarantee on this Belgium North Sea that WE will be free of ME and the agony it brings – hopefully ME can see the WE that eventually could be the most beautiful thing allowing ME to be free with the WE WE could be.

Everything is hopefully so hopefully this can be, but really… what IS wrong with me?

*The questions of doubt*:

Have I made a mistake – was I supposed to leave?
I sold my condo for this but what's it all gotten me?

Why are you noticing other girls walk by?
Is it their style of sneakers or the look from their eyes?
Could it be the cut of their blouse or even their jeans?
Sofia's beautiful, why are these girls distracting me?

Is it something new I desire or wanting to be free?
Maybe I need double D's or a girl who's six foot three?
Yet I've had all of these so what could it be?

Is it normal to think with these thoughts of confusion?
Is everything I'm thinking my grandeur delusion?
Or an optical illusion?
Am I sick? Do I need a blood transfusion?
Do you want to keep living a life of seclusion?
Is this a tactic of exclusion?
Was I hit in the head and have a brain contusion?
How do I stop this constant pollution?
If this mindset continues, will there ever be a conclusion?

Have you ever thought you aren't as great?
Simply money after a rise in the inflation rate?
What makes you think you're the heavyweight or President of the United States?
Do you really think you have all the traits?

Or that everything should be served on a silver plate?
When's the last time you even lifted weights?
Or looked at a kissing couple and didn't feel irate?
Why are you trying to control your own fate?
Would you honestly want another first date?
Where would you go and who would you take?
Why you still searching to call someone soul mate?
What about your *first* mate?

What was her name?
Why does it matter since she's so far away?
Why do you think she emailed you today?
Was your first too short and your second too smelly?
Can you even really say your third had a belly?
What about the one you thought felt like jelly?
Was it really that bad to talk with Kelly on the tele?
Why did it matter that one was from New Delhi?
Who cares if one girl always dressed like Nelly?
Did you forget another was obsessed with Machiavelli?

Are you not tired of constantly picking and choosing?
How many girls are you bruising and abusing?
Is this not confusing and losing?
Do you really think someone could find this amusing?
How could Sofia NOT be disapproving?
Maybe she seeing a sign of improving?

Improving from what? Improving how?
She can't be this good, why does she allow?
Do you really think she wants to be your Frau?
Your running out of letters, can you even buy a vowel?
Are you the type to keep your vows?

Why are you buying milk if you already have the cow?
You're eating fish, aren't you vegetarian now?
If you leave, are you planning to say ciao? Or maybe take a bow?
Or would you leave without making a sound?
Why can't you live in the here and now and just be content with everything around?

Don't you want all this shit to leave ME?
Why are you creating your own travesty?
Do you think you're a king and deserve a dynasty?
*What happened to John Lennon* and just letting it be?

How many times will it be seen…

WHAT……

THE FUCK!!!

Is wrong with me*???*

* * *

Amstel continued to write his travelling poems – some were filled with beauty and passion fueled by *burning desire*, but mostly what he saw was a pattern of discontent within his self and the relationship that had formed. He was constantly in flux – trying to determine his own love and emotions – battling ideas of doubt and confusion while forcing himself to bury his true feelings of restlessness and despair beyond the pit of his stomach. It only grew to levels beyond what he could manage – but several times within the trip a joint would be passed and it seemed his troubles would simply fly away…

No longer focused on thoughts of confusion, for in these moments he simply experienced the most beautiful girl staring back into him, happy to be with one another.

But for whatever reasons…

The next morning would come and Amstel would feel uncomfortable continuing within the same realm of beauty as the night before. Travelling through Europe in a VW for three months and some fifteen countries travelled to – Sofia and Amstel would only smoke a handful of times.

But when they did… life was beautiful.

Until eventually his reality-fluxed-confusion began to seep its way into his higher realm of being, only casting more doubt into a man that really was *filled with doubt to begin with*. The differences in his own temperament when the temperature changed, was too much of a difference to not be noticed. A question became buried within his mind: *Why are you only in love with her when you're high?*

This answer was two-sided; since obviously there was love shared when they weren't high… but it seemed even from the very beginning, Sofia's ability of breaking Amstel's own personal ideology on drugs and alcohol would be pushed beyond its breaking point, only breaking the two farther apart from a point of LOVE that must be the cornerstone of any relationship… for Amstel, it seemed HIS cornerstone was being stoned. Where even though he didn't find himself smoking on a regular basis – it was the idea of using weed to re-establish his own feelings for Sofia that brought him concern. Even though he didn't know it was bringing him concern. In the actual moment, it only brought complete and uninhibited happiness… he loved getting high and because of that he loved Sofia!

Weed eventually led to speed transforming to cocaine progressing itself to MDMA ecstasy LSD acid and pretty much whatever was presented to him – the "fun-named-drugs" the ones he had never heard of – and *when combined together* created feelings of SUPER ---- DUPER LOVE, in which EVERYTHING, even her thoughts and feelings, would be created within Amstel's own mind:

Her silent words for him:

I'm here for you, focus on me. You can be anyone you want with me. You'll know it's me speaking to you ………… You'll just know.

You don't have to impress anybody, especially me! I'm with you because of our reality together. Don't forget who you are! We are equal. You can always rest.

When you dance let EVERYBODY experience you. If you want to be watched, be watched. Just remember, while others watch you, they are not experiencing… they're watching you.

It never has to be word for word.

The deepest words are those that are shared, for me and for you. Even the deepest oceans have a bottom, I'll pull you, if need be.

# A WRITTEN SELF-PORTRAIT

You can always be alone, but not lonely. Everything you experience me as alone, is always for you! You experience whatever it is you want, you can kiss these lips forever.

You can always repeat what you say to me. always. If you have to think about saying something, say nothing. I love you.

I know you are a writer. I know you must write. If you don't want to sleep, then don't sleep. But I would still like you next to me. Your warmth, your body touching mine, you make me feel so good inside. You are simply the best!

Your structure IS the most important. I love your style.

Everything really is hopefully. Hope is stronger than belief.

Never focus too hard on the words. They come, they go. You experience them in the moment, but don't look to go back there, just know there are always new words to be found, and you find them!

After you've reached the peak, stop writing and come down. Until the next peak.

I love you.

You really don't have to speak, you speak enough, and again I really and truly love you!

Two words is good enough sometimes: so good!

When it's too much, stop. You know what matters. You never need to hesitate with me. this is who you are. Some throw the Frisbee, while others watch. You can do both. Or nothing. Do whatever you feel is right at the moment.

It's not always about me! please remember that one.

* * *

Whether it be at concert – sitting by a lake – watching a movie – going to festivals – house parties – or pretty much anything going on that week, his use of weed only helped further his love for Sofia by expanding his mind into new realms of intellect and experiencing new things *never experienced before*. It seemed he created within his own mind a pseudo-Sofia that when high, would enter his mind and calm his nerves, silently speaking to him with her words of love; until the words began to vanish.

He began to take notice of everything going on, and SO MUCH was always going on – no matter where or who he was with, he began to allow himself to *completely trip out on reality* – losing all sense and reason creating complete fantasies on *how the world works…* and most of the time… he wrote it down.

It was the pseudo-Sofia that Amstel had the truest affection for, since it seemed whenever he was in his highest realm, *his eyes were closed*; within this deepest self of his, he and she were completely free.

> Together they would roam the depths of his, discovering just how beautiful everything is and sharing their deepest affection for one another.

But then he would break away from his hidden self, opening his eyes and repositioning the world around him, hoping her eyes too would be closed… but there she was, simply staring back at him, never looking away from his eyes – trapping him in a state of hypnotic control. At first her mesmerizing stare reached deep within his fibers and pulled his true-self of dominance and power to the surface – he would grab the back of her neck and stare deep into her eyes with looks of lust and desire – never looking away from each other they became locked as one. In these moments, he would feel like god himself, only to bow down to the very *soul within the eyes creating this godlike trance.* She of course was able to handle this, only furthering their rhythmic-dance to the deepest of electronic music, spellbinding one another to the other.

But then the next moment would arise, where doubt and confusion lead to hesitation and uncertainty, only *breaking the two apart* from their locked embrace. This was caused by Amstel's inability to focus solely to her, where the wandering eyes of neighboring dancers or *even friends*, would cause Amstel to suddenly think:

What are *they* thinking of me?<br>
What do *they* think of Sofia?<br>
Do *they* think she's not the one?<br>
*They They They…*

# FUCK THEY!!!

But the thoughts wouldn't leave him. No matter how much he would try to focus his attention back on the beautiful girl sharing her love with him… the thoughts of others became merged into Amstel's mind, no longer freeing him to be what he truly wanted to be… which was *in love.*

For once you remove yourself mentally from that which gives you love, how can you genuinely be receiving that which is given to you so effortlessly, especially when your ability to receive love is taking more effort than the random thoughts from others you create for yourself who give no love.

If it was really love though…… Would I even take notice of what others think?

*Would there even be a they?*

Would there be so many questions in my mind?

Amstel constantly began to think with these questions of doubt – it was as if ALL information being received had to go through a new filtering process, in which love was no longer the filter… doubt and confusion began to take precedence and through that, even the slightest invert of a word being spoken would spark within him new levels of anxiety – over something that really was just being created within. He began putting meanings into things that had nothing to do with his relationship with Sofia – yet these meanings he created were ONLY tied to the relationship…

> He no longer was hearing what people were actually saying. Only what he wanted to hear through his newly developed negative filter. Everything said with *words* slowly began to dim his light. Until at times he found himself lost in his own darkness, unable to speak words clearly with the light that he knew was meant to shine – the light from our inner essence.

He stopped being himself – too concerned with what others were thinking of him and his relationship – he began to only say things in accordance to what he thought people wanted him to say… or *not say*.

He stopped talking in groups. Listening intently to hidden messages that he felt people were trying to share with him. From the patterns of numbers that were unfolding naturally in any given setting – to then relating these numbers BACK in accordance to his own personal number – the number that had formed within the relationship.

But what was this number he thought – what did it actually signify – and was it a personal number or that of the relationship. He couldn't wrap his mind around the idea of numbers controlling his actions – even though he understood the universe itself is governed by mathematics and we are part of this universe hence also governed by math and its fundamental outlet of numbers – yet the idea of being so closely related to all of the universe and having it take an active role in his life was overwhelming.

He would dive his mind into thought streams of fourth and fifth dimensional outlet possibilities. Understanding his own fourth, yet never allowing the fifth to form.

Each connected to each yet only understood as their separate wholes – where his forward-future-thinking of possibilities that never actually play out, would overrun his mind with possibilities upon possibilities that in the moment DID play themselves out – yet only in his own mind.

However, for Amstel – the ideas of nothing being truly related to his own self, only the self he found in the relationship, which in turn created a new self to develop, but only a self that was no longer connected to his actual self; the self-created self within his self that was actually not his true self at all – began to infest his thoughts.

He began to realize: in order to find your self – you need to be just that – yourself. And whoever he was at this point, he knew, it wasn't who he really was – or more importantly, *it wasn't who he wanted to be.*

Amstel had formed several friends throughout his travels, especially from Berlin – but it seemed they too, were not truly understanding of who he exactly was – since he himself did not know. Yet as time passed, he seemed to continually allow for these people to influence him, even though their influence was off and sometimes twisted – these "friends" of his were masters of smoking weed and taking drugs, beginning at a very early age – completely able to control their actions and reactions, speaking fluidly and coherently – in which Amstel just couldn't do – yet he was able to listen while understanding their highest of high, but it seemed he was constantly *holding back his own truth* which seemed to be counter-intuitive with some of the friends he had made from Berlin.

The words they spoke were sometimes beautiful and lovely, yet it was the strange fascination with EYES, that Amstel found himself unable to truly understand.

Maybe it was because Amstel was an only child…
Maybe it was because Amstel was without a father…
Maybe it was because Amstel had no friends growing up…

But for whatever reasons, Amstel couldn't grasp the idea of speaking directly to someone while continuing the eye gaze. This combination of speaking while peering deep into someone – combined with copious amounts of drugs – was a deadly combination for him, beginning to destroy his own relationship.

It created havoc in Amstel's mind, bringing more thoughts of confusion and doubt, where even though the words are this or that… the deeper meaning behind this and that transformed itself to something entirely different than may what have been intended.

I mean JESUS CHRIST – say what you actually want to fucking say!

> Wait…… Am I saying JESUS CHRIST from a religious stand point or more of a just words stand point? And if I say that out loud right now, what will *they* think it means? Would they think that I think that I'm thinking that I'm Jesus Christ – or the *next Jesus?* I mean, I know I'm saying it as just an expression… it's just fucking words! But do they know that? They take everything so seriously here… every fucking word has a meaning that just really isn't what's intended – and ***it's the intent that really matters…*** I mean for fucks sake, if your saying nice words, but you intend something entirely different… You're an evil fuck! Or someone who is just so insecure about life and love that you feel you have to twist even the most beautiful ideas to coincide with your twisted fucked up filter. GOTT VERDAMMT stop staring at me so much

while talking – its fucking creepy and really weird and yes it might be a cultural thing or some stupid *illuminati shit* – but it's really the *lowest level imaginable…* its medieval! It's a mindset that was formed hundreds of years ago, where none of the original ideas have even stayed true to the original purpose, of spreading enlightening values against the oppressive nature of the church… STOP WITH THE EYE!!!!

> I mean sure I get it – I understand the signs and symbols and "see" how those who can overcome the fear involved only allow themselves to progress beyond the fear – as in being *high out of your mind* and suddenly noticing a friend of even a colleague naturally block one of his eyes, observing to "see" if you can still maintain eye contact with only one eye remaining – the talks among colleagues involving owls – Harry Potter owned an owl, and used it to fight the true evil that abused the same princinples, that Harry Potter himself was following – yet based on beauty and love of LIFE, not death. The original Illuminati was only set out to discuss the love of ideas that are filled throughout the universe and cannot be found in any set book or holy doctrine.

Okay yea… you can't say that out loud. I mean, *what would Jesus do?* You know, my roommate. Well he would definitely say it out loud… I mean, he says everything out loud – that's why he's Jesus! But I'm just Amstel Jack… and *who the fuck am I?*

It was at this moment, the moment of asking himself the first level of basic questions, that Amstel knew… he had NO IDEA who he was. He was the man with the long beard – the man with long hair, intertwined with naturally formed dread locks – he was the man who it seemed people would come to for guidance. But how is this possible – how can any one man give guidance?

Guidance must come from within – not from another's within.

At festivals people would ask him if he was from Israel – at clubs, people found their way to sit by his side, asking questions from their deepest self – within his own group of friends, some would actually say, "So you're god then?"

# WHAT?!?!?

He finally is able to develop his next essay…

# I am God

"I am God." These words spoken from his lips to her ears…

*How?*

So deep in the self we actually lose our human-form which is the ONLY PLACE an idea like this can even come about – *THE HUMAN MIND*. Since no matter what level you talk about god – even at the god level, which I think it's clear to say "I AM", since I just wrote what I actually said, as the god that I AM… but even at this "god level"…

It's still HUMAN! Are you freaking kidding me?!!

How much longer are we going to be living in the dark ages of not allowing ourselves to be fully aware of the actual truth this world is about – and this truth has nothing to do with religion – it has nothing to do with god, faith or belief in a higher power… All of that is completely normal – should be accepted – and of course allowed – *no questions asked… ever!*

But the allowance is about allowing yourself as the *HUMAN BEING that you are* – the human being that we all are – *to experience the higher power* that only a human can experience. Every body of course unique and different in their own way of perceiving this *higher realm of intellect* – but to somehow just dismiss our own humanity, and believe that we were created for some purpose other than our own ideas of our own self-fulfillment is truly the most selfish a human gets.

And then to think the creation of this higher realm, the *tree of knowledge with its forbidden fruit*, is also a creation of god and not simply the natural laws that govern the universe; that we now understand at a much higher level from thousands of years ago to even be able to now call them: Natural Laws – but to somehow still think there's no truthful science in all of this – is denial of truthful science.

You are not special – I AM not special – but with this understanding creates your true special-self to flourish.

What IS special is what we're able to give back to others in our own understanding of the way the world works. But to continue our path of darkness by choosing to dismiss scientific facts will only keep us in the bubbled world that most are unfortunately still living in; where most of the confusion about our own humanity takes place. How can any human be a god?

Ask yourself one question: is it worth believing in something, if others who have believed in something different or even the same: beautiful in its idea – have been murdered. *Do you want to continue believing in the path of murder?* Because if you THINK – Jesus was murdered, and that's how he became the god that he was, if he wasn't murdered, he would have just been Jesus, the crazy Jew from Nazareth.

Really ask: is believing in something that people *just like you* have been crucified over: nails drilled deep into the palms of the hand. Been stoned: giant chunks of rock smashing into your face and knocking all your teeth out. Burned alive: where the very flesh from your bones melts more slowly than your own suffocation.

This IS religion – this is the history behind it, and why on earth would any human being want to follow such destructive ways of living. It's not needed to live a good life. If you want to believe, then believe… but don't try to understand other people's beliefs – its personal and should stay personal.

People kill others over ideas that are ALL THE SAME in their actual preached message, *which is actually a beautifully preached message of love and respect* – yet somehow people form hatred over others different than they, simply for thinking different than they…

But the only difference they're focusing on is what somebody else believes – and beliefs come from human thoughts.

Who gives a flying fuck! I'm god *you are god* everybody's a god god!

There is a god. There is no god.

It doesn't matter! Just be what you know… and let's be honest here – you can never really know god because all you can ever know is what comes in those TWO-beautifully-centered-round-balls in the middle of your face – your eyes… and what you see is what you get – and what you are in fact seeing is the life of a human being.

With so much complexity that its mind blowing – I mean, WE INVENTED GODS just to try and make sense over this crazy journey of life and death. No other species on this planet – EVER – has accomplished what we've accomplished – No other species has created these types of beautiful and spectacular ideas – that's what you call amazing.

Yet it's our fear of the unknown that somehow allows for our imaginations to run wild – to flourish – and create these remarkable ideas. It's the fear that drives us forward.

But to think it's anything but imaginative ideas is where people go down the path of murder and destruction. We all already know this, but yet we keep saying, "oh it's the past" – there is no past – there is only present – and as long as events remain in the human mind as the past yet still contemplated through thought in the human mind who is thinking it, but only in the present – the history and past of all still remains truthful today.

If you want to believe in God – YES OF COURSE! This is your right as a free-living-individual – but the moment your beliefs somehow conflict with those different and cross the paths of negativity into thinking one IDEA is better than another IDEA – this is madness.

*Let everything be.*

> Even the very idea that some will think *this idea* of either having a god or not having a god – being a god or not being a god – having religion or *not having religion*, is blasphemous because it goes against the word of god, will show humanity is still living in the trenches. Still thinking that *one* is better than *another one – it's all one! We are all one, united together through just being what we are – Human – and until this day comes, the advanced civilizations that fill the galaxy and the universe will never want to make contact with us – what would be the point of that for them? Just to feel inferior to the human species that has only made it to the moon so far – Wowwww – the moon. We're so amazing!

In the classification system of civilizations – which is measured on a scale of 1 to 3… Our advanced-technology-filled-world is still a ZERO. We're not even at the point yet to be a one – how sad is that… *we are not at the point yet to even be a one!*

Type 1: The ability for a planet to harvest ALL FORMS of that planet's resources. We currently rely on oil and coal for our main energy consumption. We're beginning to branch out into solar and wind, but in terms of overall use – oil coal and gas, is still overwhelmingly our main supply. How to fully become one on this scale:

- Wave energy
- Volcano energy
- Lighting energy
- Earthquake energy

The ability will soon come to predict and understand the *natural patterns* involved with all weather and natural forms of resources – once we can utilize them – we've reached our level one civilization.

Type 2. The ability for a planet to consume resources entirely off that planet's neighboring star. We have solar panels that are becoming used more with homes and business' – but it's nothing like powering an entire city off of pure solar energy. Or the entire world.

Imagine, at this level – energy is FREE! If the history of our species has taught us anything - it's that WAR is fought over either religion or resources. That's pretty much it. So once a civilization can reach *level two* – the complete utilization of a star – there will never be any need to fight over resources since our current star has another FOUR BILLION years of life left. I'm sure even with us taking a little bit of energy away from it, it's still has quite the ticker. Therefore, it can be understood that *level two removes war.*

Type 3. The ability for a civilization to harness energy from the actual GALAXY it resides in. It's one thing to power Earth off the Sun which is 93 million miles away – but to one day extend our reach to the center of the galaxy which is about 146 quadrillion, 742 trillion, 840 billion miles away (or 25 thousand light years) – AND harness energy from it – our current minds just can't comprehend – but the fact that we're able to at least comprehend a categorization system revolving around the idea of it – shows that one day, it could be possible.

*It's not until people can laugh* at the absurdity of our species and understand that for a short period of time:

in the thirteen and a half billion years of our universe and the four and a half billion years of our solar system and the four and a half million years of our split from our cousin primates and the couple of hundred thousand year split from our Neanderthal brethren to ten thousand years ago when modern humans began to spread themselves across the globe to the last six thousand years where written language was first created...

But for a short period of time – Human beings actually thought they were specially created by an almighty deity – which actually just shows the natural flow of science:

> Think as though every species on this planet so far – through all seven mass extinctions… from the earliest bacteria to the mighty dinosaurs and even humans… but think as though it's all just part of the *NATURAL world order*, where the *laws of nature* find themselves playing out their rules through something we call *life*. The longer life exists the more complicated these laws and rules become – slowly transforming themselves from single-cell-rules, to multi-dimension-al-outlets, until actual organisms form their own cognition of the world surrounding them. *Brains begin to form as the only way life can even understand **its own creation of itself.***

If humans were truly special and specifically created, and many believe that we are, but if this was the case… then wouldn't we be the only species with a brain?

I think even the firm-believing-creationist will acknowledge the fact that all life has some sort of brain system. Even trees – which form their synaptic connections through its roots, and have 100 trillion *root-synaptic-connections*, just like humans with neu-rons. Yet for trees, their actual synaptic connections actually connect themselves with other trees, forming a true living network of synaptic-connected-life. And even the idea that a human being has roughly 20,000 sequences of DNA and a rice plant has almost 46,000 sequences – well… what does that mean?

    Less is more?
        Quality not quantity? `
          The more the merrier?

The idea that older forms of life have longer strands of DNA, only since a process like photosynthesis, which is more complicated than our own way of consuming energy – but this process of photosynthesis is also what leads to eventually developing life that doesn't need such massive coding to survive – like a mammal.

There was a time in Earth's history where TREES and PLANTS were the only form of life on this planet. An over-abundance of oxygen then of course creates giant bugs to roam the earth, which if you focus on the structure of a bug – it truly does seem like the most logical step from small bacteria organisms finding their next cognition of life, in the outlet of bug form. Mutation mutation mutation.

Through hundreds of millions of years – continual mutations among the DNA sequences – and life's beautiful way of constant evolution, we find ourselves NOW being able to understand that there even WAS hundreds of millions of years ago… billions of years ago… infinity.

Even though a rice plant has it's 46,000 sequences of DNA – if you were to ask it how old the earth was…

Well you get the idea.

Yet without every single process of history taking its natural course in the natural order of the order in which the natural world works… We simply wouldn't be.

There is an order in this world – and it's completely *natural.*

But how do some see this – and others don't?

Why does the *vision become blurred* to the truth about our nature?

Maybe if more people experienced what in fact nature is – allowing it to become part of them, flowing through their body in whichever outlet they choose – then maybe the world would see more clearly.

*Carl Sagan, a true man of science,* expanded his mind through the use of marijuana, which is now called weed – and it's natural – it's a weed – it grows from the earth.

Now at this point – we have another divide. Since we began our "talks" with religion, then spread into science and now we've reached *drugs* – also a part of science, not so much religion. But now the divide comes in those who think this is pro-drug writing… it's PRO-EVERYTHING WRITING!

Our brain is an actual *highway* for electro-chemical reactions to take place. It's just the matter of *how many reactions* – and more importantly, in which *quantity*.

> If you have ever drank coffee WITH caffeine – I'm sorry to say or not sorry to say – YOU HAVE TAKEN DRUGS!!!

> *You have and you know you have.*

> You enjoy it and you know you enjoy it.

But then once the drug begins to cross over into the realm of enlightening – it scares most to never use again. So then you're just stuck in the level that you attained through whichever particular drug scared you, most likely weed – which if you stopped because of a fear or paranoia, that's the level you set yourself at – and unfortunately the level you will stay at – until you ALLOW for the drug – which are brains HAVE RECEPTORS FOR – targeting hormones deep within the *Pineal Gland*. In fact it's the only way a drug can even have an effect on our mind, there has to be something tangible within the brain to allow for the drug to release its natural-chemical-properties – but more importantly to ALLOW the drug to influence you in *the natural way* the drug is meant; and this is only an IDEA of one way to progress from dark to light – ***removing all secrecy of HOW to get there…………***

*It's drugs…* isn't obvious by now?

If you were to list out the names of influential people who used drugs – abused drugs – and benefited from their expanding properties – only for the expansion to be given back to the world as a new discovery – the list would blow your mind.

Pretty much everyone who has helped humanity jump forward – in some form or another has had some brief or even long-period-cycle of drug use.

Many even accredit their greatest discovery to drugs – or at least saving them from the depression many of these people faced just being the genius' they were.

*But what made them genius?* Einstein's autopsy was "reported" as having trace amounts of LSD, DMT and Cocaine.

It was Einstein who said human beings only use three percent of their brain – he of course was allegedly to use ten percent – HOW do you think? Yes – really understand the *how* behind all of this.

The whole idea of: allowing yourself to expand into new realms of thought – Without any pre-conceived prejudices that this particular way has to be the right way. *Letting your own way of truth find you* – and accept the idea that every-single-living-organism – in some way – has their OWN TRUTH… Even cows! And the acceptance and allowance of these multiple ways of truth – only allows us new heights – literally! New heights that are *not based on others* and their ideas of what it is to go high… but through the very ideas you yourself can develop for ALL OF HUMANITY – but like so many prolific people in our society – thinking in the higher realm is only possible one way…

> Let your human form experience what heights it can jump to – you may surprise yourself on the hidden-true-genius waiting inside.

> And if you're already a genius – prove it!

You have no control over where your mind goes with the use of drugs – and that is the whole freaking point! Let yourself trip out on reality – yes it's scary at first, but the understandings outweigh the fear – and *fear is only in the beginning*.

If the drug is NATURAL – not man made, but actually natural – it only follows the natural laws – this should be obvious. And if the drug IS man-made…?

Well its man made with natural substances – like psychedelics.

> <u>Nature doesn't lie</u> – the truths discovered, especially within scientific understandings, help create the new platforms next generations will stand

upon. If more people, especially those already in a natural-higher-realm of thought, but if more people allowed nature to take their minds to *even higher plateaus...* THINK of where we could be. Maybe the next Einstein would be the next Einsteins! Newton becomes Newtons and so on and so on. The truth can be scary – but accepting the truth of reality – opens the doors of your thoughts to the undiscovered discovery you can discover. But again, only to those willing to see the world for what it is: mystery.

Rediscover the mystery of life.

<u>Nature doesn't steal or kill</u> – maybe in the raw outlet of the animal kingdom, but still following the laws of Darwin – *natural* selection. And it should be obvious that we really are realms above that of a chimpanzee – yet many of the traits still remain, as our history shows.

<u>Nature doesn't preach false idols</u> because the natural world has NO IDOLS or symbols to go deeper. It is just simply the beautiful and wonderful world that if we allow ourselves to *experience a little more often* – could really take our minds *into the next realm of human thought and evolution* – and with enough people *seeing and thinking clearly*, hopefully we can reach ONE...

After one comes two

And so on and so on...

*Confusion…*

*Confusion* triggers deep into the realm of human emotion, where *feeling outweighs all thought and reason,* all words to be formed.

Yet if we understand the idea of *accepting confusion* as simply the way to live a proper life – creating within the confounds of our very own essence, our very own version of truth: only to be open to *new ideas of truth* – all based on ideas that understanding confusion is to understand that *confusion is needed for our human life.*

Be confused at times!

> Confusion leads to a pathway of new ideas. A pathway that we ourselves create – but only for ourselves.

And yes of course it's hard to accept at times of confusion – easy to accept at times unconfused. What's the difference?

It should be obvious by now – there is no difference! The only difference comes within our own interpretation of moments that are actually neutral in their truth – it's we as a species that decide what we would like to categorize as this or that – giving meaning to this and that – yet if we try and see the unbiased moments of confusion for what they really are……

MOMENTS!

Then things become clear again – our own thoughts of a situation slowly go away and the sun begins to shine as the clouds disappear from our mind – giving you your glimpse of true reality – where you again, are nothing more than the little speck among specks in a cloud of specks – and in that moment – everything becomes clear.

> These are your glimpses of *momentary genius* of seeing true reality without the interpretation of your own self-interest in mind.

Yet the moment we think of our own confusion – by thinking of the self – by thinking with the words of confusion; *all words can confuse* – confusion begins to seep back into our pores – clouds begin to suffocate the sun, casting dark shadows where light once beamed, only causing our path to seem dark.

But that's what's so amazing about this……

## THE PATH SHOULD BE DARK AT TIMES!!

Maybe if our civilization was lit by a binary-star-system, where literally there was only day and no night – okay – maybe then, darkness would seem unusual.

But we live on Earth – with one star, creating a perfectly timed day and night cycle – light and dark – *good and evil* (as ancient humans once called it). Accepting each cycle in its entirety and *not forcing an early sunrise* is the key to overpowering ideas of confusion.

When its dark – let it be dark.

> When there's light – let the light shine.

*If you can't tell if it's light or dark – go outside!*

Confusion is…

From a biological-evolutionary standpoint – what brought Australopithecus out of the trees and into the *grassland* – YES *grass*land!

From a mathematical standpoint – not really possible, since one plus one IS two and that's just the way it is – and if there's a number that makes no sense and has no frame of reference for comprehending – it's okay… *it's imaginary.*

From an astronomical-cosmological standpoint – *confusion is the area to focus on*, only furthering our understanding of how the universe works by reaching new levels of confusion, but only by understanding the previous levels of confusion; but once understood no longer stay confused.

From a neurological standpoint – chemicals – *confusion is chemicals.*

From a religious standpoint – confusion is the devil!

*Confusion is curiosity* – and although curiosity killed the cat… we're not cats. At least not in this lifetime. Maybe in the *next life* we could be cats; but after living an entire human life and suddenly finding ourselves as cats… maybe we won't be so curious… or maybe even more so curious which is what causes the death of the cat in the first place

– only allowing our next form as a wild horse or dolphin to exist:

> I mean really imagine being a dolphin – but only after you lived your entire HUMAN LIFE, *remembering everything your life encompassed,* with all the connections you've made along the way, family friends everyone – then suddenly BOOM – you're a dolphin, along with everyone else who helped you along your human journey – they too dolphins.

> Why do you think dolphins surround themselves in groups of twenty plus – and whenever a human is around – what do they do? Front flips and back flips – protecting us from dangerous predators and simply just showing us their fin, trying to say hello in whichever way they can. How *beautiful* to live the life of a dolphin – especially after living our crazy-confused-human-life – I'm sorry to say, or not sorry to say – but there's not that much confusion with being able to swim through the water like a torpedo, only to launch yourself twenty-five feet in the air, do a back flip and come down with such a splash that it only creates your Dolphin brethren to do the same – in their own way of course. All the while having your previous form of human being taking pictures of you the whole time – *silly humans, they simply have no idea that one day in space and time, they too will be a dolphin, only looking back in space and time at their previous human-species-form completely unaware of what the next levels encompass.*

Yet willing to think and believe they're always one hundred percent correct over their own creative ideas of the next levels to come – portraying itself in the *artistic outlets* each idea comes from:

> Each generation passing down through creative channels its ideas of what it is to be human and what is potentially or not potentially to come.

Why not be a dolphin?  Why not be a horse?

Or whatever you want! Or whatever you don't want.

*It's all the same…*

# Back to reality

Amstel felt relieved after writing his essay – he had so many thoughts and ideas flowing through him and his channel of writing seemed to satiate his inner feelings of discomfort with the surroundings that had formed. Amstel loved and hated the city of Berlin… love for the amount of freedom to think what you will think in the highest realm of thought, yet hate for the idea of feeling uncomfortable saying what he wanted to say, which only formed from the thoughts the environment had created, yet still never allowing a complete freedom to express what he wanted to express. Since each word spoken, had more weight than he could have imagined. People said what they truly meant, and because of that, the words Amstel chose seemed to be taken completely seriously – even if for him, they were just words.

Yes, at times words needed to be meaningful and serious – but even when Amstel wanted to talk about taking "ginger shots" for health purposes – even THESE words seemed to be taken more deeply than intended. Where follow up questions on how the ginger was prepared and *trying to understand the whole story* around the ginger shots, only created more words to be spoken by Amstel, which in turn only seemed to make everything go deeper and deeper, until his mind seemed to be *so high*, he could almost look down on god.

Amstel was not religious – he used to be, when he was a teenager – but then he smoked weed for the first time and popped his first bubble of just accepting what's told. Many of the people he had formed friendships with, were also not religious… yet they loved to discuss. It was the idea of discussion that Amstel found himself unable to take part in, since all words spoken within these discussions were meant to be so deep and profound, but more importantly – the discussions were never actually about the topic. It was more about figuring out who someone really was by the manner in which they spoke, or the words they decided to choose.

Even if Amstel tried to explain his bike…

> "Yea I like more of a slow bike, one that I can just cruise with and not have it be that complicated. But I have to just know it's my bike from the beginning. I don't want to have to fix it up or even do any work to it… it just has to be the perfect bike from the get go. Even if it's not a perfect bike, it has to be perfect to me. And even though my bike right now is the most unstable bike… somehow I find the stability within the unstable nature of my bike. I guess I like the fact that it's only a bike I can ride."

*Amstel Jack is crazy* – since even the idea of him saying this, automatically would be related back to his relationship with Sofia. Thinking that maybe since he didn't know from the beginning what his relationship with Sofia was going to be, and he wasn't planning on taking his bike back with him to California, which he had also begun thinking was a possibility of future events to take place – but he began thinking… is Sofia really the one for me, are you planning to take her back? Do you actually want a cruising type of relationship – easy going and no work needed to be done? Where's the challenge in that?

He knew deep within, the thoughts of confusion were nobody's fault but his own… yet the thoughts were always with him. Within a month of writing his "god" essay Amstel Jack would shave his beard, cut his hair, and unfortunately or fortunately, Sofia and him would no longer be together… surprisingly, or not surprisingly, it was a *mutual break up* – actually sparked by her words of "it's over."

Yet those words said were in truth caused by Amstel, Sofia was only staying true to the effect he was causing, since both knew his mindset was just too unstable to commit to a life-long relationship. At least for now…

* * *

It was the *"for now"* that would throw Amstel for his biggest loop. Even within the letters each of them wrote to each other after the break up,

"Farewell for now"

"Good-bye for now."

What did this actually mean though? Amstel knew he needed her in his life – the very thought of NOT having her would send him into a panic – where the only comfort he could find would be head buried deep within a pillow, crying uncontrollably and screaming as loud as he could with the despair of losing such a girl. Now that he was free, he started to understand he actually wasn't free – only chained to the ideas of who and what she was to him. He would find himself at night longing for the phantoms of his newly lost love.

But was it love? Why when together were these thoughts of how beautiful and wonderful she was, not keeping him grounded in the center of their relationship? Why did this happen? He truly was committed to this girl... he truly wanted to have a family with her and raise children together and live a life of love and harmony. But all of these thoughts only bombarded him once they had departed from each other's arms. Although he was free to do anything and any-body he wanted … free to begin the search for a new love – he simply couldn't.

Girls would begin to talk with him here… take notice of him there, yet he was unable to detach himself from her – she was always with him – always in the mind of a man who was now back to *square one*.

He decided he wouldn't smoke weed or take any form of drug or alcohol… EVER AGAIN! He needed to be clear – needing to know *exactly* what was going on. He slowly began to fall into a depression of hopelessness and despair. Far deeper than the pain he had felt when they were together. The friends he had made tried their hardest to break his pain by taking him to this club, introducing him to that girl – yet nothing was real for him. Even though in the moment he was present – in the moment he found himself able to speak to other girls, letting them know with his eyes he was available – yet once it crossed over into the next step, he was lost – unable to grasp the next steps. Or at least not willing to allow himself to take these next steps.

At home one night, weeks since he and Sofia had split, his roommate gone to visit his family. Amstel could do nothing but watch German TV – *trying to understand what was happening yet unable to grasp the truth of the situation.* On his roommates table was a jar filled with weed. He looks to the jar – holding it and smelling the inner confounds of the magic plant, thinking it might be time.

> Fuck it! You might be thinking you're not going to smoke again – but why are you thinking that? I think we both know, you're just finding yourself exactly where you were with Kendra several years back – insecure about who you are and afraid to be alone with your thoughts – and since *your thoughts only go to a higher level when you smoke,* maybe the only thing TO DO, is smoke again – and really just allow yourself to go there – see where your higher realm is and then filter through what you want and more importantly *what you don't want.*

You have to remember – when actually together, you just weren't in love with her – if you were, you would still be together. And of course it's hard to grasp and accept this, since it really was so easy to be with her – but at the same time, it wasn't that easy to be with her – since you yourself really didn't want to be with her. You only wanted the idea of her and that's why as you sit alone, only having your thoughts and ideas, the pseudo-Sofia takes hold of your mind. You have to let it go… sit back, roll a joint, and watch a movie or something… allow yourself to be free – for both of our sakes.

Yet as he smokes his joint, with his personal bottle of Irish-blend-whiskey – all he can think of is *family*. The ideas of being a father and what it actually means in this world to take such a path, having a child call you "daddy." Everything becomes related back to her: how she's the one he'll have a family with – how she's the one that could allow for a higher level of love. Although its good-bye *for now*, he still envisions her as the one he'll have it all with – and these thoughts, built and forged in the highest of high… make him happy! He begins to create scenarios of coming home to her and their children – picking up his son and smiling deeply to Sofia with passion and excitement. He imagines himself surrounded by his friends, laughing and playing games together, having the greatest of times. Yet as his high begins to dim, he suddenly understands: *all of this is only in your mind.* If it can't be like that in reality… then what is it really?

A fantasy.

This fantasy only broken by Amstel's sudden thoughts of others – how some of his friends would think it would be the wrong choice, or that the moment he would say they were back together, it would be awkward. *But who are they to even decide?* But it didn't matter, whatever Amstel tried to do, he continually would begin to think of others… a slave to their approval and what they thought of Sofia and his relationship to her – even though he knew NOBODY ever understood who she was or him for that matter, or more importantly what she was FOR him – especially his friends from Berlin – since they never hung out together as a couple, only Amstel with his friends – Sofia with hers. But everything was always within her circle – her groups – and even the groups Amstel had formed for himself, really weren't his, since everything from Berlin was formed through her.

At times Amstel just wished they were able to live in California, get married in Vegas and not give a shit – Los Angeles was beginning to cry for him – and he began to listen.

He hated himself.

But he would soon began to realize that the friends who's "approval" seemed to be a disapproving approval, was actually a representation of *his own disapproval* – since there wouldn't be these disapproving ideas of doubt and confusion coming from his friends unless HE WAS THE ONE who was actually in doubt and confusion… if he was truly happy with his relationship, the same friends of his, with the same words spoken, would be speaking different things – it's only within Amstel's own mind that the words twisted themselves – and that was because she just wasn't the right girl for him. Which was the most painful thing to think of. But it was true.

He hadn't experienced what lasting love is – and to continue his thoughts of longing for what is now only a fantasy would be counter-productive to the growth he needed to endure, to finally allow himself to receive and more importantly *to give* his deepest of love, something he just hadn't done yet. The only way for him to maintain his sanity would be if *he really is the one* deeply in love – since it was within his own mind that all the chaos and mayhem took place – he needed someone to give everything too, knowing deep within, THIS would be the lasting love to last – freeing his thoughts from even thinking about his own thoughts – if he had to think whether it was right or wrong – it was most likely wrong. *When it's right – you just know.* There's no wrong when it's right.

And sadly, Sofia just wasn't the right girl for him… at least *for now.*

*Or maybe not* for now.

∗ ∗ ∗

A 5/5$^{ths}$ possibility is always ONE. For after understanding the idea that although the chosen path within the fourth possibility within the confounds of the fourth dimension, but only understood as the future possibility of only ONE actual path, lived out in the present-third-dimension self, yet only understood within the future-fourth-dimension-self… ONE begins to understand that even the idea of wanting to understand the idea of a *fifth* dimension understanding, ONE must do just that… understand what the fifth dimension actually is, since there's no way to break into the fifth – where all possibilities of all possible choices takes place, unless one is willing to sacrifice the understanding of the future fourth which is lived out in the third.

Therefore any path chosen BEFORE the fifth dimension is understood is technically a limited path, since the only way a fifth dimension understanding can take place is to understand that you're fourth dimension self is only a later version of your third dimension self – hence being no different in what possibilities actually take place – all possibilities in the fourth are already decided, understood and experienced as reality once you're third reaches that point in time – hence feelings of a routine life become the focus when choosing the path that is the already chosen path – which WAS the fourth.

Only the fifth will bring the unknown aspect back to life – feelings of confusion, excitement, instability and all other lost emotions within the fourth, become the focus in the fifth. *Nothing is known in the fifth dimension* – and that's what makes it worth understanding.

Anything and everything is possible within this dimension – even better understandings of your own fourth can become clear – yet it's only through a full acceptance of reaching the fifth where clarity becomes clear – hence needing a genuine letting go of all thought-idea-feeling still tied to the fourth dimension.

*If the unknown is what you desire – the unknown is where you must go.*

# Numbers

One-eight Spaniard on his mother's side – *four/fifths Deutsch* on his father's - a two/thirds combo of three-and-a-half Indian tribes on his mother's father's side – and a three/sixteenths combination of combining a quarter Jewish on all sides. Amstel Jack never understood the numbers – in fact, he hardly understood ANY number before he left for his great adventure through the world. The first number he would begin to understand was the number four.

*For* it was on his *fourth* day of travelling, still in California, that he would meet Sofia – sacrificing his ideas of India and living under a tree, to begin a travelling experience with her. Even though he knew she would not be the one to save him – he also knew she WOULD be the one to save him – and open him to a world never seen *be-for e*.

Once in Berlin, after a year of *experiencing* and finally being accepted by those who truly were the heart of Berlin, the numbers would begin to unfold: starting with the downfall of the number three and Hitler's Third Reich – for as Amstel began to understand more and more, in which all conversation was only in German – it was clear that if the choice of three or four was given – FOUR was always the number chosen – for obvious reasons. Unless it just had to be three, in which case, subtle laughs would echo from those understanding the deeper meaning behind the choosing of three.

Amstel himself had his own version of a fallen third – for it seemed whenever the number three was presented, Amstel would find himself thinking of Kendra. Even though she had no actual significance to three, Amstel thought that maybe it was the fact that she was the third girl he had connected with, which would make Sofia his fourth. But as he went deeper with the numbers, other girls would begin to blossom in his mind – showing him the number scale was off. Maybe Kendra was not three, since they never actually had a true relationship – *at least not yet???* – maybe Sofia herself was Four making Amstel unaware of his own number. Yet at Festivals, Sofia would wear a shirt with the number five on it – potentially representing herself as five, or maybe to show Amstel he was her fifth connection.

As he continued to live in berlin, it seemed pretty clear, that while Sofia and Amstel were together, his number really was four – at least that's what everyone thought and presented to him.

If the group was waiting for the bus, which *always had a timer*, someone would look to Amstel and say, "hey, four minutes!" smiling deeply to Amstel, trying to encode his mind with the idea of four. Triggering deep within him that his path with Sofia was correct since he himself was now the essence of four and in this exact moment being shared, FOUR is the only number to see or understand.

Amstel was lost with all of this.

Another friend of his, constantly would show him the famous Berlin graffiti of 1UP, which is scattered through-out the city. Its actual meaning: *life* – yet with the numbers constantly flowing through Amstel's mind, he could only assume it potentially meant 1UP from his own number of four meaning five – which he could also relate to Sofia since it seemed she represented the five quite well, yet it seemed all numbers must be taken personally.

Amstel's own passcode on his phone: 5555, which he chose since it's in the direct center of his phone and he wanted to remain centered. Yet one evening, a close friend of Sofia's – *beautiful in her hypnotic way*, noticed the passcode and said, "Oh hey, that's a good number for you!" even though she KNEW Amstel had already attached himself to four, only triggering deep within, his need to go higher on the number scale – she of course smiled deeply and *lovingly* to Amstel once he connected that idea – as if she was read-ing his mind, trying to guide him to a new path – a path Amstel thought she wanted to be a part of; only casting *darker shadows of love* in his mind, where the sharing of her favorite book, involving a love triangle, would resonate deep with Amstel. Who now began to think two women were in love with him – and *two should never involve three.*

Yet he couldn't change the number on his phone, since that would be accepting the idea that this *numerology* running deep within Berlin was true – so he kept his 5555 code and tried to associate it back with Sofia: but once a bubble is popped – its popped.

A simple graffiti tag, of a random name with four dots, triggered differently with Amstel than if there were three. Apartment buildings and store front cafes… ALL SCATTERED WITH NUMBERS – each of them entering his mind and causing more chaos and doubt, bombarding his mind with confusion: 35 – where's the four? 14 – is actually five! 45 – could be a joining of the two each represented, yet as he looks across the street… 1UP is seen, making 45 the process in which 4 becomes 5.

After the two of them parted ways – the number four still had its weight – But FIVE was slowly beginning to make sense – as Amstel begins to accept the truth of what the truth actually is…


The Fifth Dimension.

# Epilogue
## Amstel begins to write



*<u>The silent teachings of the zig-zag</u>*

To those w out love...
I see the expressions on your face
The pain the sorrow,
Listen to the melody,
No past or tomorrow
Then you see the feeling is there
Waitin to be found
It's not about you, let's be fair look around
They are everywhere!
open your eyes to the world around you
Let people in. Let people out
They come and go no rhyme no reason
With the gentle call of one of the four seasons
Summer winter autumn and spring Living in the moment, now you see
What you see has no words
With no words comes no thoughts,
It's the secret of living
The secret life she brought

To those who cannot reach their higher stream
Close your eyes, then you will see!
With eyes closed no enemies or foes
patience is virtue, eyes shut to continue
It's not about you!
Distractions arise when one thinks of the self
The self must be lost, like a book on the shelf
The shelf of the self, where self turns to shelf
Lose the book, forget the shelf to free the self
Do not be distracted!
eyes closed to take it all in
realize there's never an end.
No alpha no omega
No me you or I
With eyes closed you are given a surprise
As gentile as water as warming as fire
The stream itself will always get you higher
Don't be afraid of how high you go
Fear is your enemy, the only true foe
Let the stream in it fills to the brim
Never overflowing, essence of a true friend
It comes and goes, there when in need
Never suffocate, it's alive and must breath
So I say to those who cannot reach their high stream,
Sometimes a flower must turn to a weed

I once sat by a river w a man named Joel
He was a wise man because he knew he didn't know
What he didn't know he knew
And what he knew he didn't know, he knew he didn't know
I sat w him for a while and pondered his thoughts

On life and love our inner voices became crossed

And it was then that I realized the mistake of his ways,

He had taken the path alone, and for that there was no grace

But alas, his friend, had the courage to ask...

How is it that you've removed your innermost mask?

However, just like him, I also knew nothing, until I stopped sitting by that river, then it all turned to something, suddenly it came to me and it was all so clear, the path to serenity was gently blowing in my ear, I awoke from my slumber, no more need to close my eyes, and it was then that I saw the gentle tear within HER eyes. And that tear quickly told me exactly what it was, it was the very same river that we ourselves were upon. I quickly jumped in and left everything behind, then life's greatest gift leaves nothing to surprise, it's greater than a prize, surreal to the eyes, never masked w hidden lines, or dubious cries,

its the magic of her water

And it's magically alive


Don't record the words spoken to your child,

Those words are sacred, those words should be wild.

Wild w the knowledge you've acquired through the years,

Wild with the knowledge that you've suffered with tears

Not from the books you've read or films you have seen,

They'll experience all of that, remember, you were once a teen

Read to them the pages that's composed of your life,

And bestow upon them some of your greatest insights

Never should, always could, and one day would

This will lead to life's protective hood

Cautioned and be warned, this next part gets tricky,

For if your insights are wrong, it tends to get sticky

Tangled like a helpless moth full of knowledge,

Ready to be eaten, abandoned and lawless

Love should be the only insight that is given

All other ideas deserve to be eaten

So if you want your child to make an impact on the world,

Teach them three virtues that haven't been told:

Plants have life, since plants can die

What's written is only written, and therefore can be a lie

Write your own book, and never disguise, the thoughts feelings and emotions that all is comprised

just so you know, the three virtues are yours, the deepest of which will come knocking at your door.

Everyone has in life there own three virtues,

The task we take is to find them and continue.


Realize and embrace the beauty of the world

Around and around, it's spiraled, it's curled

Never straight is the path one takes,

but from your perspective it's always straight

You yourself are the essence of this beauty

Don't be afraid, it's the way it should be.

Release it openly as one always should

But only when realized experienced and understood

Then you have begun the path of the spiral, atoms galaxies and universes, the flow is undeniable


I feel so blessed to be here

Here in the now, here in the present

Present is gift – Gift, given to all who want to receive – Receive is easy –

Easy as giving –Giving to those who should be given – Given to those who should receive – Receive is to understand that those who are should are also those that could and would – Would, if only for a moment

Moment, for the should could and would.

That is the understanding – Understanding of the now – Now, what to do – Do nothing – Nothing is all around.

The beautiful ways of the should could would fold together into the unfolding fold that folds only for the very fold that unfolded it
Backwards and forward is complicated, like the fold, therefore stay in the center, where there is no fold


To those who know the now,
Now has three letters but only one centered vowel


When in doubt, close eyes
If no close
Ask why.
Eyes close way to feel whole,
reason you came,
let self be soul.
Have trust people you not know,
let witness you,
become greatest show.
Don't try force think.
Close eyes and sink,
then see,
everything infinity
Life death all same
Why sad, of course change:
Pine cone to tree, tree to stump
Close eyes, get over hump.
Realize miracle miracle life
newly embraced husband wife
Make love together, create other life, task of wife, creator of life, beautiful wife, give life, wife is life, life with wife.
Growing old beautiful
Death true miracle
Age only relative

dying is regenerative

It's because of her I can be who I want to be, sit the way I want to sit.
I can be in a high chair, leg the way I want it, foot where I please.
It's because of her I am a king today
It's because of her I'm a man today
A knight
A traveller
A warrior
A lover
Of course a lover!
Deep with her until the end, living w her and willing to bend
No fear in the heart no doubt in the eyes
Life turns to death, always ready to die
Not to escape or relieve my misery,
But because I understand death is our greatest mystery
To embark upon that path w love in the heart,
Means I've done something right and will get a new start
Nobody can know where the start begins,
But to even begin again means there's truly no end!

When I dance, I let others experience me
Never do I infringe on others
because I dance for me!
Eyes closed, then I see,
that those I dance with are part of me.
They might leave and dance somewhere else,
But with eyes still closed,
There is no where else.
Everyone stays, yet everyone goes,
My face with a gentle smile,

That's how I know!

Don't think... Just dance!
The time and place to watch fire,
Only when built, to experience growing higher.
After you witness the dance of the flame,
It's time to look deep and see what's within.
Caves and caverns, lava flows under bridges,
The inner world is hot, and seems endless,
You become entranced in this magical form,
Until you realize it's just one of four.

There's always time to watch beauty
Watch the way it works
Watch it's flow
It's grace
It's innocence
Look at beauty in all it's glory and know...
It's yours, smile
You have beauty in your life, smile
Smile smile smile
You have beauty
You have LOVE
love
Such a beautiful word
Such a beautiful way
If everything were made of love
Then we could all just know
We could just know it
The secret
And understand it

And embrace it
And live it
Which is what love is
Just live love
And be love
And love the fact that we Experince the way we can
Not like animals, or like any thing else in this universe
We Experince it like humans
Equal and lovely humans
All the same... All connected
And connected to that very essence and force that gives us this life
It's love.

There's always temptation
In all shapes and forms
it comes in different directions, usually out of the norm
Is left right?
Is right right?
Which way is up?
Which way is down?
Can someone please tell me, I'm all turned around!
And once I realize I'm confused
I understand the good news:
The right path is not confusing!
Is a river confused?
The bristling leaves of a tree confused?
I think not
To be confused is to be wrong
There is never confusion w the right direction, the right path
Do not be confused
Break through the confusion to the truth

bad or good
It doesn't matter.
Why You ask?
Because once broken through you'll realize the truth, a correct path is
never confused

How did I find her?
Always an appropriate question to ask one who has found
I have found.
But I had to leave my old ways behind... I had to leave
To the unknown
And not looking for her!
My quest was india to live under a tree for 6 months eating fruit
But I am open
Open to new ideas and new paths
And when I saw the right path befoe my eyes... I went for it
Already committed to her from the beginning
Her eyes, her lips, her body!
She unfolded for me, and I folded to her
We danced, we played, we made love
We did it all, well, what was permitted in a 3 foot high tent.

This is such a magical place
You have to see the magic
Then embrace it
Become it
Know it
Love it
This is such a wonderful place
Full of wonder
Full of the unknown
Yet, in the unknown is the known

The known of love
The known of mystery and intrigue
Do not ever be deceived
Embrace
Embrace what you don't know
And in turn, you embrace the known
The known to survive
The known of life and beauty
The known of love
The place is filled w it
Be filled

Like a newly formed tattoo, looking wet, as if it can be dissolved
But it can't
Looks can be deceiving
See through the deceit
To the permanent
To the concrete the path forms
It looks wet, looks disolvable
But it's not
It's this essence of permanence that gives strength
Strength to be who you are
To experience what you choose experience
Experiences are the only path to concrete forms
Experience a Tattoo, in all it's glory
Become permanent w it
Then you will see the finite within the infinite cosom of the branded
Become branded
Become that which you fear
But don't fear it
Love it

Appreciate it and uphold it
It formed you, and in turn, you form it

What are you waiting for?
A redundant question turned rhetorical in our lives
But once truly asked,
The answer is true
Don't run from it,
Embrace it... It's our calling!

Have the confidence to be who you are
Through her, you are created
Its she that gives you this life
This love
Don't run from it
Always embrace what can potentially make us run
It's this running where we become free, it's the running where we come from
Like a child, running as fast as he can, no goal in mind, no objections...
And hence no obstacles
Run free!
And be who you are

Always come back to the melody of the stream
It grounds you in the moment
It's built of ground
A stream isn't water
A stream isn't nature
A stream isn't a creek or a river.
It's the purest of sounds which come in many forms:
I went to a concert w the music of my choice becoming free in the moment
it was then I heard its voice so clear and elegant the way of true sound

how is it people have learned to make such a frown for it's music that
creates life's great mysteries music is the deepest of the streams inner most
intrigue

beautiful is the fact tht we ourselves can make it,

composing day and night stripping ourselves to be naked

For once we have removed all of our said clothes,

It's then the music teaches what we don't know

It's only for a moment and it's only a glimpse,

But in that very second infinite time exists

Break through the third dimension into the fourth wall barrier

say hello to your audience for there is no such greater

Music is sound, sound is stream, music is as simple as the simple
sound-stream

Even through this verse which is musical words, the words having
melody, the words creating beat:

From the heat of the street meets the discrete sound of musical concrete

Built in your mind from the very time when a line could decide whether
to rhyme or squeezed like a lime

Sour in nature still with flavor to be used like a favor make sure to savor
for there's honestly nothing greater

Sometimes but a sliver and be a good giver

Gifts made w intention no apprehension or sense of hesitation never w
indecision or procrastination but w a lovely aura of loves calculation

one plus one can be three

But only if you believe


It's all because of her


The outside always rots

It's the inner which you desire

You must tear back the bark and behold the beautiful color the wood hides

Even the most burnt and charcoled piece, can be cleaned and stripped
properly, to become fresh again, to the eyes

The forbidden fruit, the apple, was meant to be eaten

I only knew Leço for a short period of time
Dread locks to his waist, the musical game was his rhyme
He danced and he grooved letting the music fill his soul
He replenished what he took, never feeling a hole
As quickly as he came, he vanished from my journey
To the next man w dreads, I'll be sitting, I'm in no hurry

She talks and i listen
I talk and she listens
Never impeding w thoughts about the self,
Never concerned w anybody else
It's the way to communicate in the highest form,
Sometimes what we talk about is other peoples form.
Their troubles their worries and how everyones in a hurry,
We even talk deeply over some rice made w curry
Beyond our words which sometimes get confusing,
We have the ability to remain quiet, no longer discerning
Away to our world and focused on the self,
It's there we recharge and replenish ourself
Until the next time we decide to go deep w one another,
Let us rejoice in the now for we know there's no other

A tree that splits into four different parts:
Three from front and one from behind
You need connection, like a dog without, he just sniffs and wonders not
knowing what's its about.

Why speak negative words
What if someone is listening, what if someone thinks it's teaching
Your words of negativity, weigh down like ruling dynasties.

Not lord or master not even a sir,

Drop the formality, it makes people concerned.

Concerned w the idea you think it's deserved,

Deserved is a word, a word that brings concern.

But if you're equal to the beggar and thief upon the street,

Then join the drum circle, even but for a week.

In that week you will clearly see, how connected we are, and the beauty we all seek

For beyond the search, our goal should be happiness.

The problem comes when you think you know, tht others should partake in "what you reap is what you sow,"

No judgement or hatred for those opposite your view, if that's how you feel, then the path is askew


Have you ever wondered why you are alive?

I don't know if you've noticed, but others have died.


A state of paranoia means you feel you're being watched,

Go back to the beginning,


Use a fucking crosswalk!

Were words once uttered

How stupid I was

As if I could decide where people choose to walk!


You have to read your own poetry to come up with your own title


You're truly experiencing the moment when you haven't realized you're at your destination.

And you're truly at the right destination when you don't realize it's your destination!

When someone talks they're no longer silent.
Have you ever pondered that

Certain titles should sometimes be given
But only to those which there's a love, this way noones blind

THE TAO TE CHING, book beyond words, within book, inelegant words: true words false and false words true, understand nature, UNDERSTAND TRUE. seems wrong, not right, no sense, no right, no rhyme, yes rhyme, no matter, WORDS RIGHT. truth easy, easy truth, difficult read, difficult need, tiny seed, larger tree, sometimes leaves, sometimes breeze, Tao Te Ching, MUST READ. Change life, life changes, good and bad bad and good, all same, NO DIFFERENCE, let happen, happen needed, everything beautiful, once understood, understand difficult, DIFFICULT GOOD. Want easy? Easy why? Easy easy, no try, try good good try, nothing easy, THATS LIFE. look harder, harder reads, read hard is hard read, Up is down and down is up, right is left and left is right, life is death and death is life, all this change, is changing me...
Simply be, THE TAO TE CHING

The knowledge of unknowldge is the main subject here,
Come to think, I think I went there!
Here and there such a beautiful phrase, it was definitely a trip But it was definitely a phase.
Like many of the phases in life we are continually encountering, most leave us lonely and most leave us lonely.
The true phase in life will most definitely begin, realize who's who... And Love her to no end!

Balconies everywhere!
There's something magical about the balcony away from home,
You just have to experience it,
There's no words to be written on it.

Low means high, and of course high is low,

Practice what you preach, the preachings of the unknown

And w this comes the idea that you actually do know, what you know
you don't know, and that's all you really know.

To know is to unknow, and that's the first step to knowledge, the knowledge of the unknown, the knowledge to unknowledge

So feel safe with the knowledge that you don't know this knowledge and
embark upon the path ... The secrets of unknowledged knowledge


You can make so much last if you don't consume it all


If your going through all this work, you better sit there!
Relax and enjoy


I forget how warm you are:
But it's nice you can remember it again!


To people who want there voice heard...
Good, voices need to be heard.


A simple acceptance of a flyer, reminded me of a time when I handed
out the flyer.


Poetry is the expression of absolute truth... The harmony of balance
The harmony of truth


Not against police, just against the policeman
The policeman, like the nazi, taking orders and doing what's told
The police itself is only trying to uphold


Theres a rhythm to a chant, otherwise it wouldn't be a chant:
No borders no nations, stop deportation

Don't pour out what comes in a bottle

Have you ever danced freely in the streets?
If not, maybe your on the wrong street, maybe it has the wrong beat
You always could change your street... Listen to a new beat.
People dancing next to you, side by side
Every thing is fine, for nobody tells a lie
Expressions on the face never decieve
When confused on the new street, watch a dancer, feel their heat

So many simple and subtle things you can find:

**purple blue butterfly flapping yellow spotted wings.
Crimson red rose releasing its sweetest scented pheromones.
Long blades of the greenest green grass, scattered buzzing bumble bees of future present past.
Golden streaks of beautiful yellow lit sun rays, piercing through puffy clouds, with a distant smell of rain.
Sounds of children laughing-playing with the innocence of youth, baby birds chirping-beckoning waiting for mothers food
Newly paved bike paths with giant trees along the way, the simple sound of a skateboard means today is a good day.
A soft unfolded blanket laid gently upon the ground, eyes closed lying back, ready for natures sounds.
People around with the same idea each with a unique smile, my dog is panting out of breath, no need to go into the wild.

I sleep next to that which is beautiful the curve of her body the softness of her skin, what could I have done to deserve this akin

Beyond the gentle blowing in the ear there's something deeper that I know,
It's that I'm always free to be myself, and that's as deep as I can go.

To free your self to be your self is the glimpse of loves musical rhyme
And the miraculous thing to understand, is you can go back there anytime.

No such thing as a tree w too little light,
If you look at the tree removed from distractions it's right
Take out the view of the over other trees, and see the unlit tree for its
individuality

Continually writing, expressing a moment,
Only a glimpse, enough to conjoin it.
sacrifice then your indulging ways,
To jot a few lines and slowly fill your page.
Back to the moment you must go
To understand what's next...
forgetfulness as a foe.
Carry on carry on, find a way to write something,
Even when something turns to nothing,
At least this nothing came from something.

When you immerse yourself in a crowd of people,
You sometimes miss what's meant to be discovered on your own

You create what you want,
You see it,
You feel it,
That's it.

Don't just warm you hands by the fire, WARM your hands by the fire

You must be able to face every fear you've ever had, and accept them as
possible truths,
If every fear is possible, and you accept them, there is no more fear
behind the fears

Go the brink, then break it...
That's how you progress
I went to a brink, and broke it.
I know there's more to come!

There's no need to hear how people met... As long as they met, that's great
enough.

Be able to say one thing, with a simple meaning, only to instantly go deep
on it, and find its also a good deep meaning.
I can't move.
But in a good way.
Deep.

There is only good and bad.
Things can be great, and that's good.
Good is always great, that's why it's good.
It's all just so simple at times.

I think I'm a Buddhist

This is so amazing!
If there are two exploding lights, pick one, then watch it completely.
When it goes out, watch the other ... Until that too goes out.
Then you feel complete.

Don't think you have to keep your lighter in your pocket.
But sometimes you do.

If you want the truth behind a question, ask yourself why you are even
asking it in the first place.
Most of the greatest answers never even had a question!

Someone once told me they figured out Mona Lisa's smile,
When I asked how,
There was no answer.
It was amazing!!!

Find your answers from above, eyes open to see. It took closed eyes to
get there, but once there...
Open!

Up is high, down is low.
You can be low, but still high
And you can be high, and still low.
They are the same. Up and down is the same.
That's all you really need to know.

What is the zig zag?

The question I asked, as the question I feel hasn't been asked.

The greatest discoveries come from questions that none have asked. Then
the answer is completely yours. You make the answer...
And they do have answers,
To those who ask.

Asking is the most difficult.
We feel that we need to be so sure of ourselves all the time.
It's pride. And being proud is like being a lion ... Only, your not a lion!

My favorite Freud quote:
Sometimes a cigar is just a cigar.

The order it goes in, really is the order it goes in.
Trying to control the order is the same as trying to control the order.

Trust your natural order.
Trust there's no control.

Don't look for your next incredible experience.
Let it find you.
That's what makes it incredible in the first place.

What is using "it's like" like,
It's like you're always trying to make a situation clear to others, while making it clear for yourself.
It's like the simplest form to every situation, is like the way we can show ourself it's truth being spoken.
It's like, truth is what we seek,
And to be able to have a situation unfold so clearly,
Into a NEW situation, is like one of the greatest experiences.

You don't have to act out a situation.
Unless... You want to act!
Then commit fully, until the act is finished. Then stop acting.

When introducing someone special, to someone special...
What makes them special?
Put it as simply as possible.

I would rather understand the words,
Than actually speak them.

To look directly with another requires a trust.
So it's good.
Learn to trust.
To not look directly,
Requires a different trust.

Learn different trusts.

Incredible laugh - incredible love.
It sounded the same...
I heard incredible love.

Sometimes you just have to trip out,
So then later, you no longer trip.
All that's left is truth.
And it's amazing!

Why are you here if you're not going to experience it.
Only do things when you're ready to experience, other wise don't do.
If you're not willing...
You are not open!
If you're not open... You are closed.
No access to help.
No access to be helped.
Every one of us needs help!

Always receive gifts, and appreciate them the way they were intended.
Otherwise, accept the gift, and give to someone who CAN appreciate!

We must always hydrate.
Especially when its offered.
Always when it's offered.
Unless you're not thirsty.

Never ask why someone hates.
Just don't speak.
Those words don't deserve words.
They will learn.

Or they will die.
They will learn to love.
Its always love.

Death is only fear.
Always face your fear.
You will conquer it.
We all do.

Everyone has different fears.
Again, we are all human.
It's part of who we are.
Don't ever fight what you are.

The problem for some of us:
Once we leave,
We still feel we are connected to where we left.
You can only connect to the moment.
It's as simple as...
1, 2, 3... 4-5-6!

Being alone is the easiest thing one can do.
We are born alone,
We die alone.
But those two are just doors!
Don't live the in between standing in the door!
You know?

Learn from a mathematician.
Learn how NOT to be a mathematician.
But only from a mathematician.

You don't NEED to give,
But always give!
Unless there's nothing to give.

How can the sea become greater than the ocean?

The sunrise will never meet the sunset.
Both equally beautiful.
However, if they did meet...
Well, that's for you to decide!

Amstel is no poet.

Let us continue, shall we…

Sneak Peak, Chapter 1

a written self-portrait

"On Tragedy"

# Chapter 1

As the head began to lower in the slightest show of respect, Mantuko began to absorb. Crossing dimensions into the physical realm was easy compared to understanding what each physical cue represented… and more importantly, the information needing to be extracted. The problem was he had zero idea on either.

*A king from a different dimension.*

The very fabric of what created a life, simultaneously creating a king, was a foreign concept on this world. The individuality of each individual to feel as though they were individual was an idea for further understanding. Do they really think they matter? Mantuko understood the meaning of a world: simply put, he knew a world when expressed physically was a home. It was unfortunate that for him, his endless stream of inner worlds – each larger than a hundred universes – would continue to be kept within.

As Mantuko continued to look at the man, dressed in some formal uniform (multiple pins and badges across the chest) his head beginning to raise from his slightest of bows – Mantuko outstretched his arm toward the man and simply said, "DOWN." Within an instant the man, who Mantuko now realized was a general within the army, was face planted and stiff as a board on the concrete steps of what He now knew to be the capitol building. The information began to flow:

MILITARY SIGNAL:

slogans – slow-guns. bearing of arms – weak. technological advances within the last 50 million years — one. scale set at infinity minus one.

language – vocal and written – 6,000 languages protocol reset.

mathematics – multiple symbols represent. line circle triangle square sphere to cube.

geography – boarders on land. open ocean.

history – not enough information: aggressive with war.

culture – based on number of people, expansive -- drawings. music. food. clothing. dance. literature. film. celebrations. country.

religion – ideas of god or gods.

Science – counter intuitive to most ideas. understanding limited, based on basic flat mathematics.

politics – ideas of democracy.

humanities – ideas of altruism, many live without.

family – based on blood relations.

friends – based on similar ideas shared.

money – needed to survive – disproportionally set, option to earn.

education – set to adult year of age – freedom after, many continue.

markets– capitalism based on a company economy.

legal system – strictly enforced at *almost* all levels – ideas of privilege.

race/ethnicity/gender – one of biggest conflicts for entire planet.

animals – roam planet without law, habitats dwindling.

resources – becoming scarce: global warming set. dependent on the lowest forms of energy. wars fought. population struggles. denial.

type of civilization — not even level one, scale set to fifteen.

This would be easy.
As the general began to pick himself up off the ground, looking around in utter confusion, unaware of the force that made him split his chin, Mantuko raised his arm again. Sensing the blood from the general's fall, Mantuko knew the command and did not hesitate to use it, "TO ME".

With tissue in hand, trying to stop the blood flow from his face, the general froze in complete non-action. His eyes fixated forward with the blankest of expressions. At this point, there were already several people around the general, looking to help him and make sure he was okay. But the power of the dimension is strong, and by simply touching the general, those around him also became fixed in place. The command of TO ME was beginning to take effect, as the blood from the general's chin began to globularly form an orb around his face, growing as it drained the life from his body, suffocating at the same time. Within seconds, a towering man of authority was left emaciated and withered on the capitol's steps.

Mantuko fluttered his fingers as the blood encompassed the others still fixated in a lifeless trance. Like a spear thrown from the greatest of giants, it penetrated them, obliterating their bodies, leaving only orbs of blood.

The screams beginning to spread throughout the streets were silenced to gurgling-white-noise as a minutia of *red* began to enter their open mouths, most standing fixed in place, unable to break free. The very moment someone saw the mayhem or heard a scream it was too late. As the policing force began to enter the scene, weapons in hand looking for the culprit responsible – Mantuko knew it was time to see their capabilities. A potential saving grace.

As the final blood was drained from those without weapons, their bodies almost mummified sacs of dust-like-chalk, the policing agents seemed horrified. Many unwilling to leave their vehicles of transport, some on talking devices, others with weapons drawn – pointing out in all directions.

Mantuko's quick surveillance of the scene allowed him to know instantly the chain of command and cowardice. Here was this planets' protective agency and they were unable to identify him and had ZERO ideas of what was going on. The very fact the general was so easy to take down told Mantuko this simply was a planet unaware of the importance of truth and their ideas of royalty and honor were dwarfed only by their own hubris of induvial self-care.

As Mantuko closed his fist, the blood orbs joined together around the vehicles, which Mantuko knew were of metal making, and instantly crushed them to the size of his own fist. Police still inside. The remaining armed police began to scream and run, finalizing the belief of what he now knew FOR SURE was a wasted planet.

A planet of people living life only to serve death. Creating ideas and beliefs that although some were of science and fact – most only served the agent of death that seemed to overtake all of those who believed in it … which Mantuko knew, was everyone alive at this very moment. This was a mistaken lost planet; a planet of pride and greed and forsakenness to the actual truth of who birthed the life of planets in the first place. Wrapped up in their own self-inflicted ideas of what they *thought* was pain and misery; feelings of sadness running through the very core of the planet's life source. Fire and brimstone couldn't remove the disgust Mantuko had for these people of multiple faiths and ideology and lowest level of intelligence (and as training, Mantuko sat in fire for 5,000 years). These were a people of factions – divided nations – false idols – weak militaries – basic concepts – lonely hearts – disregard for others – a planet of beggars and kings, neither of which were true – a planet of NEED – a planet of me vs you – a planet of sinners only defined by their own definition of sin – a planet of helplessness – a planet of hopelessness - a planet of FAKE – a planet of killers rapists and thieves – a planet of corruption – a planet of boredom – a planet of SICK – a planet unbalanced – a planet tilted – a planet that was just OFF – a planet lacking knowledge – a planet lacking wisdom – a planet lacking the ability to change – a planet needing more and more – a planet ungrateful – a planet unappreciative – a planet gone wrong!

## "INITIATE ANNIHILATE"

As Mantuko began to elevate himself off the ground, the now marble sized vehicles began to spin around with the orbs of blood becoming one. higher and higher Mantuko began to rise, while the iron within the blood joined with the metals of the marble police vehicles, becoming smaller and smaller in size.

"SINK"

A blurp of light no brighter than a candle, and the entire planet was sunken into nothingness, not even a black hole as a reminder. Mantuko's last image of the planet, which he loved to store within his own consciousness, was more of a thought than an image: how could an active planet, with more than seventy percent ocean, billions of different life forms, be so out of touch with truth. On to the next…

$$e^x = 1 + \frac{x}{1!} + \frac{x^2}{2!} + \frac{x^3}{3!} + \cdots, \qquad -\infty < x < \infty$$

As Marinthica walked toward the altar, her precious newborn in arms, a sudden shudder spread throughout her body. The divinity of the *Devine Church* seemed incomparable to the love she already felt for her child. An innocent reflection of her deepest soul, untainted by the years that marked her life and the countless stories of oppression she knew ran rampant in the colony. She was one of the lucky ones. Born with a high-birth status and given the intellectual capabilities to determine her own self-worth, she knew she shouldn't have complaints. Yet, looking at her son; his eyes fixated on hers – she couldn't help but worry.

As she glanced around the *Divine Church*, with its ever-encompassing presence of the Holy Water: holographic liquids continuing to penetrate the millions of people in attendance – she already knew the Oracle would have to make a sacrifice.

It wasn't out of the ordinary when a high-birth baby was born to need a sacrifice. Even when the paupers gave birth to their non-birth low-ranked children, a sacrifice was always made – it was mostly the *manner* in which the sacrifice took place, and more importantly how many would be needed, that seemed to always worry the mothers.

When Marinthica was born it was said throughout the colony a chosen child would give birth to THEE chosen child, and only a TRUE chosen would lead the worlds to the higher realms. This was Marinthica's fourth child, the previous three all receiving the needle.

As she approached the Oracle, the only one within the colony allowed to wear blue, Marinthica suddenly got the urge to break protocol and look the Oracle in its eyes. Not one person in the colony was allowed this privilege, not even her father's father – who in fact gave birth to the Oracle. The previous time an active Oracle was within a colony was more than a hundred thousand years ago, also birthed from a high-birthing male.

As their eyes locked, Marinthica's violet to the Oracle's white, the Oracle lifted its arm to stop her and the newborn in place while releasing a shriek that began to echo throughout the massive chamber of the *Divine Church*. To some, the shriek was nothing more than the calming sounds of the Holy Water, but for those who had fire within – it began to shock them at their core. Convulsions intertwined with uncontrollable spasms began to spread like wildfire amongst the people. Those running toward the exits were halted by the Oracle's gaze, as impurity within the Holy Water was being flushed to the collective minds of all high-births; now locked in trance, breathing in unison with deep guttural sounds, eyes fixated on the oracle.

As Marinthica looked to her baby, only a flutter of white appeared within the eyes before the baby shut them with the force of a thousand locks.

A new oracle had been chosen.

As the thought entered her mind, a single tear across her cheek, she felt a presence unforetold by the ancient histories. The teardrop was becoming alive. Slowly growing and beginning to drip-drip-drop onto her baby – the truest of Holy Water giving its blessing to her and her newborn, now named Oraka: first of the male-line-heritage of Oraka Oracle.

A silence began to take effect, as those convulsing slowly burst into flame – releasing millions of years of generational knowledge. Each particle of light visible throughout the *Divine Church*, dancing its way to Oraka; sizzling as they touched his now tear laden body. Within moments, Oraka's eyes began to flutter as the information of ALL-LIFE continued to enter his body:

Mathematics, languages, sciences, technologies, cultures, religions, creativity, music, loves, hates, peace, wars, defenses, attacks, beauty, ugliness, what to die for, what to kill for, what to live for, friendliness, kindness, meanness, spritualties, trust, lies, honor, strength, weakness, sacredness, impurities, Holy Water, *Divine Church*.

As Oraka began to open his new-born eyes, Marinthica couldn't understand the very next moment, when she was suddenly on the ground and looking at the Oracle holding her baby and gazing deeply into his eyes. The guttural chant still emulating throughout the Divine Church, yet solely coming from the Oracle and being focused heavily into the eyes and mouth of Oraka. The Oracle held the baby – white eyes to white eyes — forehead to forehead – breath to breath – sharing to receive and receiving to allow the share. The oracle began to shrink, her remnants of body liquifying into the Holy Water while intermixing with the particles of fire-light still entering Oraka, the sizzling sounds matching the tones of guttural chants. As soon as Marinthica was on the ground bearing witness to this, the oracle had already vanished.

Oraka was in a puddle of flame – and he was rapidly growing in size.

"i am i am."

◯

Mantuko's eye, centered on his forehead, was pulsating white. A complete reflection of the emanating energy flickering deep within his mind. Purities of shimmering light essence kept within – protected and secured – looking to be released.

"YOU ARE YOU ARE" He whispered.

As he continued to sit, third eye piercing the very fabric of nature, his remaining left-right eye were switching between open-close. Like a telescope using different lenses to gain clarity – Mantuko was intrigued. He was still learning how to maneuver and understand the capabilities of a physical form. Granted, at this very moment he was a representation of ALL physical forms in ALL understanding, yet — the knowledge of *which is which* and more importantly *when is when* was something never experienced before. A new sensation began to arise, something he had never felt – even the idea of *felt* was foreign to him – but at this moment, as his third eye began to reabsorb into his brain and his body began to put all joints-bones-muscles back into place – he felt a spark of joy.

○

"Sooo … What do you think?" Amstel asks.

"it's really good, I like it." Ramona says, her head nodding ever so slightly. "It seems like a good beginning with a pretty interesting idea for a story."

"But can you see how I can NOW incorporate my thesis into this?"

"Definitely. I assume this oracle child will be like, the *poster child* for your thesis?" she asks, almost rhetorically, still nodding her head.

"Well … Yes and no." Amstel replies, taking back his computer from her lap.

"What do you mean?" she asks.

"Well, I haven't decided if I want to focus on this child, and what it means to be born with TOTAL KNOWLEDGE … like my dissertation suggests, or Mantuko, and his ability …… oh wait … is it '*HIS*' ability? Or '*THEIR*' ability? Whatever, it doesn't matter …… MANTUKOS' ability– there it is. Nailed it!" He laughs, and continues, "but yea, I still can't decide between the two – eh, maybe both."

"Well … it sounds like you know." she says smiling back.

"I know I love you."

"So, you love <u>me</u> then?" She playfully says, yet still waiting for his confirmation.

Amstel looks deep into her eyes, penetrating her soul with fire that only grows when they both know the exact moment to let it burn. He begins to caress her inner thigh, his fingers delicately moving up her soft skin until he reaches her pleasure. Her face shows the emotion she feels deep within – every touch he gives intensifies her deepest longing for him – a simple touch sending her into writhing ecstasy, where even the slightest of penetration has made her convulse for hours and hours of pleasure and pleasure and pleasure and pleasure. She's insatiable.

"Amstel! HEY, Amstel ……………… AMSTEL!!!
I'm not going to tell you again … Lights out!

Do you hear me, Amstel?! AMSTEL!! ---------- get outta the corner man! HEY!!! DO Y0U HEAR ME? I'm getting the nurse if you don't go to bed … AMSTEL YOU LISTENING TO ME?!?! HEY! What are you doing in the corner??!!"

"I'm writing I'm writing I'm writing I'm writing I'm writing I'm writing I'm writing I'm writing I'm writing I'm writing I'm writing I'm writing I'm writing I'm writing I'm writing I'm writing I'm writing I'm writing I'm writing I'm writing I'm writing I'm writing I'm writing I'm writing I'm writing I'm writing I'm writing I'm writing I'm writing I'm writing I'm writing I'm writing I'm writing I'm writing I'm writing I'm writing I'm writing I'm writing I'm writing----------"

"Get the nurse call the doctor … I think he just broke his years of silence."

# About the Author

From the corporate world spending $30 on buzz cuts to traveling through Europe in an old VW with naturally formed dreadlocks - Louis Gale has lived a life. Only because he chose to die.

When the moment of choice to jump off that cliff came — it was an owl and hawk that saved him. Even the bugs growing multiple generations in his hair wanted him to live.

We die when we are meant to — Louis was meant to live — for now.